T0246740

IN THE FACE OF

CATASTROPHE

IN THE FACE OF
CATASTROPHE

How a Traumatic Brain Injury
Became a Blessing

JENNIFER ROSE GOLDMAN
AND CARYN MEG HIRSHLEIFER

GREENLEAF
BOOK GROUP PRESS

The names and identifying characteristics of persons referenced in this book, as well as identifying events and places, have been changed to protect the privacy of the individuals and their families.

Published by Greenleaf Book Group Press
Austin, Texas
www.gbgpress.com

Distributed by Greenleaf Book Group

For ordering information or special discounts for bulk purchases, please contact Greenleaf Book Group at PO Box 91869, Austin, TX 78709, 512.891.6100.

Design and composition by Greenleaf Book Group and Sheila Parr
Cover design by Greenleaf Book Group and Sheila Parr
Cover image © Shutterstock/cla78

Publisher's Cataloging-in-Publication data is available.

Print ISBN: 979-8-88645-208-2

eBook ISBN: 979-8-88645-209-9

To offset the number of trees consumed in the printing of our books, Greenleaf donates a portion of the proceeds from each printing to the Arbor Day Foundation. Greenleaf Book Group has replaced over 50,000 trees since 2007.

Printed in the United States of America on acid-free paper

24 25 26 27 28 29 30 31   10 9 8 7 6 5 4 3 2 1

First Edition

This book is dedicated to our inner circle—to Mischa, Jenn's loyal, loving, and dedicated partner; to Amanda, Jenn's sister, best friend, and Caryn's Sunshine; and to David, Jenn's father, hero, and Caryn's adored husband.

———

This book is dedicated to anyone who has suffered any kind of neurologic condition or disability, as well as to the doctors, researchers, and scientists working tirelessly behind the scenes to advance the treatment of such conditions.

———

Finally, this book is also dedicated to those who have had to work to overcome adversity of any kind. Your stories continue to inspire us.

ACKNOWLEDGMENTS

Thank you to everyone who has helped support our family through Jenn's life-and-death struggle, her ongoing recovery, and the writing of this book.

To Jenn's cousin Rob, Rachel, and Alexa, who saved Jenn's life that August morning.

To Jenn's aunts, uncles, and cousins, whose love and patience in times of fear and hopelessness have eased the way.

To fellow employees of Hirshleifers, who share the memory of that fateful August 2021 day and who have welcomed Jenn back with love and open arms.

To the excellent doctors, nursing staff, and therapists at North Shore University Hospital and Glen Cove Hospital, and specifically to the staff of the NICU at North Shore University Hospital, whose extraordinary care kept Jenn alive.

To the incredible Dr. Henry Woo, Jenn's neurosurgeon at North Shore University Hospital, who brought Jenn out of the darkness and back into life.

To the excellent Dr. Sarah Khan, physiatrist at Glen Cove Hospital, who has skillfully directed Jenn's recovery.

To Susan, Frank, Jen, and the other physical, occupational,

speech, and vision therapists who have been with us every step of the way.

To Saul Katz, Dr. David Chalif, Dr. Jared Cooper, former congressman Steve Israel, Greenburgh Town Supervisor Paul Feiner, Rabbi Michael White, Rabbi Ilana Schachter, and others who generously reached out to us in kindness, and provided advice and support at critical moments. We are so grateful.

To our dear friends who've stayed close, prepared meals for us, baked cookies for us, and made their presence felt in many different ways—you know who you are.

To our home health-care aides—Shanelle, Marie, Elvie, and others—who have cared for us like family—we can't thank you enough and couldn't have done it without you.

To our focus group of readers who have given their time and attention to reading and critiquing the manuscript.

And to the incredible team at Greenleaf who has guided us and brought this work to fruition, including HaJ Chenzira-Pinnock, Adrianna Hernandez, Morgan Robinson, Lessie Schrider, Sheila Parr, Karen Cakebread, Chelsea Richards, and Gwen Cunningham.

CONTENTS

PROLOGUE

A massive bleed in the left frontal lobe of Jennifer Goldman's brain left her comatose and clinging to life on August 18, 2021, just days before her thirty-first birthday. As a result, each member of our family was forced to grapple with Jenn's potential sudden death.

In the Face of Catastrophe: How a Traumatic Brain Injury Became a Blessing is so titled to reflect Jenn's deep gratitude for having emerged from her unconscious state. However, this was a collective experience, so it's fitting that our story be told through a narrative that includes the firsthand perspective of each family member as we navigated this crisis.

In the pages that follow you will hear from five primary narrators:

Jenn, a wellness entrepreneur and dynamic motivational speaker who lost her ability to think and speak through her stroke and is still in the process of recovery.

Caryn, Jenn's mother, an attorney and part owner of Hirshleifer's Inc., who writes alongside Jenn and plays a pivotal role in the book's genesis.

David, Jenn's father, an experienced board-certified emergency physician, who struggles to balance his roles as father and physician.

Amanda, Jenn's younger sister, who takes on the role of Jenn's advocate and protector.

Mischa, Jenn's boyfriend and now fiancé, a newcomer to the family who chooses to step up rather than step away.

You will also see other voices and perspectives join the story to recount the impact of the traumatic event, mostly in the form of written communication and documentation.

Told chronologically in an interwoven narrative, our voices carry the reader through the emotional highs and lows we experienced as Jenn vacillated between life and death, struggling to triumph over her right-sided paralysis and severe cognitive deficits. The different storytellers demonstrate the broad reach of one shocking moment in time.

This time in our lives has shed light on the existential issues we each face. We discovered what it means to be present in times of uncertainty and crisis while holding on to hope. We have learned so much about the power of family and community to sustain us through these challenges. In this memoir, we hope to share some of the wisdom we have gained in the face of our own catastrophe, finding glimmers of blessing along the way.

1

PRESENT DAY

Jenn

My brain died a violent death on an otherwise tranquil Wednesday morning in August, just three days before my thirty-first birthday. I woke up feeling fine and meditated for close to an hour before driving to work at the store, a retail business owned by my mom and her sisters. When I got to work, I felt strange. The next thing I knew, I couldn't walk straight. When I tried to speak, the words made no sense. And then my head exploded. A searing hot bolt of pain ripped through it as blood poured into my left frontal lobe from a cavernous malformation I didn't know existed.

Like a Rocky Mountain spring snowmelt rapidly destroying everything it touches, a cerebral hemorrhage severed my neural pathways, connections, and memories, leaving me comatose and clinging to life. The bleed was so intense it took more than ten days, three intracranial drains, and an emergency craniectomy to stabilize me. For three weeks, I floated in and out of fentanyl-twisted consciousness while my body lurched, fighting to stabilize without a functioning autonomic nervous system to do the job.

The relentless drone of machines and people coming and going all night make up the little I remember of the next three weeks in the neurosurgical intensive care unit (NICU).

2

THE STROKE: AUGUST 18, 2021

Caryn

Jenn's mother

At 9:15 a.m., I got a text from our general manager: *Call me now. Jenn's not right. She's walking into walls, like she dropped acid or something.* Jenn was into wellness. Herbal supplements, yes. LSD, no. I was gripped by fear.

My husband, David, a board-certified emergency medicine doctor, was off work, so he immediately left to check on our daughter. Moments after he left, our manager called me; her panicked voice was overshadowed by a deafening, bloodcurdling howl. Then another. And another. Though the sound was primordial—like a prehistoric animal being gored—I knew it was Jenn screaming in agony. I dropped everything, jumped in my car, and raced to her. My heart pounded.

As I drove, David sent a text: *Jenn had a stroke. The ambulance is here. I'll wait for you.* His words, too terrifying to absorb, bounced around my head. I arrived moments later to Jenn being wheeled out of the store on a stretcher. She looked unreachable and miles away, like she had somehow left her body. She was a shell of herself. A wave of panic ran through me; my stomach was caving in. *Am I strong enough to handle this?* I wondered.

The store staff followed Jenn's stretcher out the door to the ambulance. They congregated in small groups, sobbed, and hugged each other as the EMTs loaded her in through the rear doors. They kept the engine running, ready to receive her before rushing her away. While I couldn't process most of it, I knew the traumatic sounds and images would linger in everyone's minds. Everyone there that day was now bound together by this horror.

David

Jenn's father

My drive to the store was terrifying. I kept my hazards flashing as I ran through red lights and stop signs like a crazy person. I had to get there and see Jenny. I tried to think of less-upsetting reasons Jenny might be in bad condition, but inwardly I knew she was seriously ill. My attempt at denial was just my mind playing tricks. I was angry with myself for not telling Caryn to have the manager call the ambulance, stat. In retrospect, it wouldn't have stopped Jenny's brain bleed, but they could have at least begun stabilizing her intracranial pressure.

Jenny was on the floor in a dressing room when I arrived—moaning and pulling at her hair with her left hand. Her face was distorted. I couldn't believe my eyes. I made a hopeful joke to assess her mental status.

"Jenny, if you wanted to take a day off, there are easier ways to do that."

She didn't respond. I lifted her right arm and let it go. It dropped without resistance. I lifted her right leg. Dropped. She was having an acute intracranial bleed.

"Call an ambulance. She popped a vessel in her brain," I told the general manager, who was standing next to me in the dressing room.

She dialed 911. I could hear as the dispatcher started asking questions. I became frustrated.

"Tell them it's an acute intracranial bleed and we need an ambulance NOW!" I shouted, then quieted and said to myself, "My daughter is critically ill; she's in unbearable pain and there's nothing I can do to help. I'm a doctor, but there's nothing I can do. I feel so helpless . . ."

I had to get outside. I couldn't stay in the room with Jenny. I couldn't look into the eyes of everyone who was looking at me, trying to gauge how bad things were from how upset I looked. Things were very bad.

"Speed it up! Get the ambulance here!" I called out to nobody as I paced in front of the store.

The ambulance arrived in five minutes, but it felt like an hour. Two EMTs lifted a stretcher out the back and carried it into the store. Everyone stood around in shock. Caryn arrived, just as Jenny was being wheeled out.

Jenny's condition had worsened. I could tell by her body's decorticate posture—hands clenched, elbows contracted, arms tight against her chest—an involuntary response to significant injury. She needed the pressure inside her skull to decrease as soon as humanly possible. I was terrified.

They loaded her into the ambulance and slammed the doors shut. The siren blared and she was on her way. Caryn and I followed, speechless during the ride. Four words ran over and over in my mind: *Jenny, please don't die.*

Caryn

David and I had no words for one another on the ten-minute drive to the hospital. We were together yet very much alone, awash in our own thoughts.

In my mind's eye, I saw Jenn as a young child, blessed with striking physical features. People often commented on her full, perfectly rounded lips and her strong, angular face, likening her to some fashion model. Perhaps her physical beauty drove her to prove she could be otherwise accomplished. There was an intensity about her, a perfectionism that led her to set high standards, overcome challenges, and circumvent roadblocks. As she grew up, her perfectionism gave way to negative self-judgments. Jenn became angry, sad, shut down, and increasingly dysfunctional. She was drinking excessively, cutting class, smoking a lot of weed.

We intervened. Early one March morning when she was in eleventh grade, two escorts transported her to a wilderness program in the Blue Ridge Mountains of Georgia. She didn't know they were coming; she would have run away if she had.

In the presence of nature, free from negative influences and distraction, Jenn rallied. She emerged from the experience emotionally grounded and aware, with a deep understanding of life many people her age didn't fully grasp. People saw her inner light and were drawn to her. The embodiment of tenacity, grace, and resilience, she became a source of strength and inspiration to others.

Straight out of college, Jenn started a wellness business focused on inner (rather than outer) beauty. She became a motivational speaker on self-care and wellness, started a nonprofit, created an online course, and more. She was passionate about her work, extremely independent, and adventurous. She drove herself all over the country for yoga festivals and other wellness events.

I started to call her Lady Arachnida because she was like a spider to me. She wove her beautiful web every day. When part of it tore or was stripped away, she simply rewove it. No complaining. No regretting. Just moving forward. Her tenacity was inspiring, and I was so proud of her.

Her humor was one of my favorite things. A hysterically irreverent badass, on her nana's ninety-second birthday she left a voicemail saying, "Hey, Nan. You're getting kind of old, but you're sharp as ever. You have the attitude of a boss, and you are a queen. Sending so much love today and every day."

We shared so much, but at that moment in the car, I didn't even know what tense to use when I thought about her.

Northwell Health Discharge Note to North Shore University Hospital, 8/18/21

This is a 30-year-old female who presented to North Shore University Hospital as code stroke for gait instability, right hemiparesis [partial paralysis], and slurred speech. Last known well at 10 a.m. on 8/18/21. Patient was at the store where she works. She was noted to suddenly not feel well. She was walking "wobbly" and then went down. Did not hit her head. She was kept on a couch by her coworkers and noted to have slurred speech and right-sided weakness. Her father came immediately after being notified by staff and they called Emergency Medical Services (EMS) stat to take her to hospital. En route to Emergency Department (ED), patient had an episode of aspiration and began to have extensor posturing per EMS. In ED, patient required intubation prior to imaging due to mental status and prior to intubation noted to have tachycardia with extensor posturing concerning for another seizure. Prior to intubation noted patient having anisocoria [unequal pupil sizes]: left pupil 7 mm and right pupil 4 mm. Patient was transported to Neurointerventional Radiology for a selective cerebral angiography to determine a source of hemorrhage.

Amanda

Jenn's sister

I stared at the text from my dad.

Mands, Jenn's not feeling well. Come to ER at North Shore.

I was completely freaked out. My body careened into full fight-or-flight mode. My heart began to pound. My palms started sweating. My breath quickened. My thoughts raced with the absolute worst. I texted Jenn's boyfriend, Mischa, when I was stopped at a red light on my way to Jenn. I told him to come.

The family knew how traumatized I was by my own stay at North Shore. I knew they wouldn't tell me to meet them there unless things were very bad. Several Augusts prior, my car was hit head-on by another driver who suddenly veered into my lane. I had no time to avoid the oncoming car in the milliseconds of terror as the distance closed between us. I'll never forget the violent explosion when his car hit mine.

My car flipped and rolled. Metal twisted; glass flew everywhere. I landed upside down with seat belts hanging from what used to be seats. Sheer adrenaline moved me out of the car and through the shattered side window. I didn't know it, but my back was broken. I was airlifted to North Shore University Hospital; I was taken to the main trauma room in the ER. When Jenn saw how broken my body was, her face was stricken with terror. And here we were back at North Shore, the same month, in the same ER. But Jenn was in the hospital bed this time.

There was so much running through my head that it felt like my brain was going to explode. I took it all in—concerned looks from the nurses, paging over the loudspeaker, code calling, shock and horror on my parents' faces. My accident, my trauma, was suddenly, vividly back. And because of this, only I knew what awaited her. I suddenly understood how hard it must have been for Jenn to see me, crumpled and shattered, all those years ago.

It's my responsibility to advocate for her. It's up to me to carry her through, I thought.

When we were all gathered inside, they told us Jenn was very, very sick. Her brain was bleeding. Only a few months before, my best friend Jake had died from an undetected brain bleed after a car accident. How was it even possible that Jenn, just twenty months older than me, had a brain bleed too? It didn't feel real. It couldn't be real.

What will life be like if I lose my only sister? I struggled to understand.

Mischa

Jenn's boyfriend

As I was about to walk my dog, Shadow, a heart-wrenching text from Jenn's dad popped up on my phone: *Call me, please. It's an emergency.*

It was the second message I received that morning. The first message was from Jenn. Our birthdays were only a week apart, and she wanted to get our upcoming celebration plans in order. Jenn takes birthdays very seriously. Last year we had celebrated together for the first time, and the day did not quite live up to her expectations. I promised her we were going to do it right this year.

As soon as David started talking, I was thrown into shock. I could not process what he was saying as he tried to explain the situation. I heard "ER" and "a bleed in Jenn's brain." Time froze. Jenn's life was suddenly up in the air. I sped to the hospital. Amanda texted me while I was on my way.

When I got to the ER, Amanda was the first person I saw. Caryn and David were already inside with Jenn. Due to COVID restrictions, patients were allowed only two visitors at a time. Since her parents were already there, the staff told us we were not permitted inside to see her. Amanda lost it. She was so vocal about needing to go in that the hospital asked the social worker assigned to Jenn to intervene with us.

When the social worker came outside of the emergency

room and saw how distressed Amanda was, she let us inside. From that point on, even though Jenn was supposed to have only two visitors, they permitted the four of us to be present by her side.

After fighting our way through the COVID restrictions, we found ourselves waiting in a small side room off the lobby. We were both in the dark—literally and figuratively—and we were both drowning in a swirling whirlpool of thoughts and feelings. Hours of painful, traumatic chaos followed. The reality unfolding in front of me was incomprehensible. My shock grew deeper and deeper. There was nothing I could do for her.

The doctors did not know what was going on. Every update filled me with despair. All I wanted was to hear she was stable, that she was going to be okay, anything good, but each piece of new information seemed to be worse and more uncertain than the last.

I prepared for the worst. *I need to hold Jenn again*, I told myself. I clung to this thought like a lifeline. In this storm of uncertainty, this was one thing of which I was absolutely certain.

Caryn

My heart ached for Amanda. As excruciating as this was for everybody else, I knew it was unbearable for her. Amanda was born with heightened sensitivity to the environment—noise, lights, temperature, even fabric—and was easily overtaken by such sensations.

Observant, intuitive, and a deep thinker, Amanda is an empath who takes everything to heart. Her feelings hit her like a tidal wave and drag her out to sea for days sometimes, isolated and unmoored. She can be incapacitated by pain, a physical symptom of the trauma her body absorbs. Often, when she rediscovers balance, she is ashamed and remorseful for her sensitivity, though there's no reason for her to apologize for how her brain is wired.

Last year was particularly difficult for Amanda—she and her boyfriend broke up, she moved back home from Boulder, Colorado, and her best friend, just thirty years old, died two months before from an undetected bleed in his brain. Now the same thing was happening to Jenn.

I could see Amanda quietly decide it was her job to advocate for Jenn.

This is too much for her tender shoulders. Does she know what she has taken on? I worried. However, I knew there was no dissuading Amanda. She was going to take care of her sister.

Our time in the emergency room was terrifying. I could literally feel the fear and urgency of the staff as they worked Jenn up. At some point, David stepped out to make a few calls and I was left to stand about awkwardly. Quiet, intense, and purposeful, the staff offered no smiles or words of encouragement. It felt like they didn't want me there; things were too touch and go. They needed to focus on Jenn, not commiserate with me. I was a distraction, which somehow made me feel even worse than I was already feeling. Their silence underscored the seriousness of her condition. Every few minutes, an announcement came over the hospital loudspeaker: "CODE STROKE. EMERGENCY ROOM."

It filled me with dread.

Eventually, the staff ushered me into a side room, where I took a seat. I didn't want to speak to anyone. I tried to make my body smaller, pulling my arms tight into my torso, shrinking down into the chair, hoping I would become invisible. I needed to disappear. I thought of the book *To the End of the Land* by David Grossman. One character, the mother of an Israeli soldier, left home when her son was recalled to active duty so she could not be notified if he was killed. I was trying to do the same thing.

After an hour, when David returned from his calls and the hospital finally let Amanda and Mischa join us, we were taken to the interventional radiology unit's family waiting room to meet Henry Woo, the doctor assigned to our case.

"Your daughter is very sick. She's in a coma," he said, brief and direct. "There's too much blood to see what's going on through scans. I am going to do an angiography, and that will tell me more."

We stared at him in collective silence, trying to take in his words. We found out later the emergency department had to intubate Jenn before they attempted imaging because of her diminished mental status and a dangerous heart rhythm. There was so much blood and pressure to mitigate, they inserted a drain into her brain.

"Just so you know," he continued, "this could be a clot in her venous sinus—with multiple bleeds. If so, the prognosis is not good. I'll know more in about forty-five minutes. I'll do my best."

My breathing quickened. My heart raced. I began to tremble uncontrollably. I tried to take deep, grounding breaths. *Intake, hold, one, two, three, release, one, two, three, four.* My vision constricted until I could only see directly ahead of me. Amanda sobbed. David sighed deeply. I just wanted to tune it all out.

Amanda

Is my sister going to live? I need to see her. I need to be with her.

Time stood still as we waited for Dr. Woo to do Jenn's procedure. I was flooded with memories of my accident. I smelled gasoline and burnt rubber. Twigs and weeds were stuck in my hair. I was dragging myself through a broken, upside-down window. I was flying in a helicopter. I was lying in this hospital where I now waited for my sister.

A photo came into my mind. The two of us standing side by side in our Power Ranger costumes. We must have been eight and ten. We had just gotten home from trick-or-treating, and we were posing with our candy-filled plastic pumpkins.

Another memory flooded me. Jenn presenting her thesis on the "subtle body" as a college senior with a double major in religion and philosophy. She stood tall at the lectern, clearly in charge of the material and the classroom filled with teachers and students who came to listen. She was so confident, poised, graceful, and beautiful. She had a huge smile on her face. She knew she had crushed it. Though I had absolutely no idea what the subtle body was or why anyone would spend a year of their life studying it, she was magical. I beamed. That was my older sister. I was so proud of her.

Jenn and I were always there for each other. And she needed me now more than ever before in our lives.

David

Multiple bleeds, coma, Jenny is very sick, bad prognosis. Dr. Woo had just sent us all to another world with his words—a world where he punched us over and over. I had to rally the troops because we couldn't bear the stress. I couldn't bear the stress. We needed something to take the edge off.

As the medical professional in the family, I went into analysis mode to save us. Dr. Woo was doing the cerebral angiography, which meant he was likely an interventional radiologist. As a radiologist, he wouldn't necessarily know the neurologic implications of what he was seeing. *Woo could be wrong,* I realized. *Thank God. Woo could be wrong.*

"Okay, everyone. We can disregard what Dr. Woo just told us. He's not a neurosurgeon, so he doesn't know for sure. He could be wrong," I said immediately.

And for the next few minutes, we relaxed, but only slightly.

Dr. Woo appeared at the door no more than five minutes after he had left for Jenn's procedure. Amanda jumped. Caryn began to cry. I shook my head. We all took his sudden reappearance as a bad sign. Obviously, he had started to study her brain and stopped because she was too far gone. I sighed, slowed my breathing, and sank into a depressed acceptance, preparing for what was coming. *We are going to lose her.*

"I have good news and bad news," he began. "It's not a clot in her venous sinus. Thank God. My hunch is that it's a cavernous malformation. If I'm right, I will hopefully be able to remove it."

It turned out he was a neurosurgeon after all.

"The bad news is that time is of the essence," he continued. "Any rebleed will likely be fatal, but I can't remove the malformation until the blood drains—and there's so much blood. We have a long way to go before she's out of the woods, and anything can happen. Step-by-step, though. We'll get there."

I exhaled loudly and relief filled my body. She could have been driving, at the beach by herself, or walking in the woods when this happened. Instead, she was at work, and we were able to rush her to one of the best neurosurgery departments in the New York City area. I understood her survival was uncertain and she could decompensate at any minute, but we were so lucky.

North Shore University Hospital Department of Radiology Report, 8/18/21

> *There is a large left frontal cingulate gyrus and corona radiata hemorrhage measuring 6 cm in anterior-posterior diameter by 3.4 cm transversely with extension into the left lateral ventricle, a cavity in the brain that contains cerebrospinal fluid. There is also intraventricular extension into the right lateral ventricle, third and fourth ventricles. There is mild hydrocephalus [swelling of the brain] with dilation of the temporal horns.*

Caryn

We sat huddled together in the waiting room as they readied Jenn for transfer to the neurosurgical ICU (NICU) on the fourth floor. It felt like hours. Amanda and I held hands. I could see David's silent tension in his posture and the distracted look on his face. He sighed periodically as he likely considered the gravity of Jenn's medical state. Each loud exhale unnerved me.

This must be grueling for David, I thought, imagining the competing demands he must be feeling. Doting yet grieving father, physician who knew the full weight of the possible medical outcomes, and family medical advisor gauging what we could bear to hear. Sadness was a hard emotion for David. A lighthearted, warm, outgoing, spontaneous man, he also held a deep melancholy from unresolved past hurt. Like a bullet lodged deep in his chest cavity, it was too close to the heart to operate on. Sorrow could set off an avalanche of prior disappointments. And when this happened, he would retreat into an inner space he created for himself where I couldn't reach him.

I knew there were things he wasn't telling me. I knew it was unfair that I could maintain blind ignorance while he bore the heavy truth. But I was too scared to ask.

My heart ached for him.

David

Jenny was alive and we were really lucky, but the more I learned about her medical condition, the more I worried. She had a cerebral vascular accident (CVA) and was paralyzed on her right side. Her right arm, hand, fingers, leg, and toes could not move. The bleed site was in her left frontal lobe, the part of the brain responsible for emotion, personality, and higher thinking skills like empathy, attention, self-control, and memory. The part of her brain responsible for thoughts and speech was the most damaged, and I was stricken with fear.

There was nothing more important to Jenny than her ability to think, to write, to connect with people. These traits were her core, and I couldn't imagine her losing any of them. Every minute blood remained in her brain, the potential for irreversible brain damage increased. *If she survives, who will she be? What will she be left with?*

I kept this all to myself; I was already concerned about how Amanda and Caryn would react when they finally saw her in the NICU. Without a working brain and functioning autonomic nervous system, Jenny would have temporarily lost control of her heart, breathing rate, body temperature, blood pressure, digestion, and metabolism, among other important systems. She would be hooked up to so much equipment to perform all those functions for her. She was going to look a mess.

Even with everything I knew, I was shocked when I finally saw her in the NICU. Tubes and IVs seemed to be coming from every part of her body. A tube in her throat regulated her breathing. An IV line ran from a large vein in her neck so she would receive fluids, blood, and medications without delay. There was a catheter to control her urine flow, a nasogastric tube to carry food and medicine to her stomach through her nose. There was a frontal ventriculostomy catheter in the right side of her skull to drain the blood from her ventricles. There were so many beeping monitors I stopped counting. Her hands and legs were in braces.

Despite the plastic and metal, the whirring and whizzing, she was so tranquil, so beautiful. She lay at an angle in the dark room except for a dim light shining on her face and the glowing screens of the many machines. After all she had been through, my baby was alive, at peace, and resting comfortably. She looked like an angel.

For the moment, that was good enough. In fact, it was a miracle.

3

NEUROSURGICAL ICU

Caryn

Jenn was finally moved to a room in the neurosurgical ICU (NICU) late in the day. The urgency in the unit was palpable when I walked through the doors. The staff spoke with purpose, activity was constant, machines hummed, and alarms sounded frequently to signal anything from a low IV drip to a patient crisis.

The nurses looked at me knowingly, as if they could see all the challenges lying ahead of us. The wary look in their eyes scared me the most, forecasting the many ways everything could fall apart. I couldn't help but feel they were sizing me up, assessing if I was strong enough for what was to come . . . as if I had any choice in the matter. Like David, they knew things I didn't know, and even if they were willing to tell me what we all faced, I didn't want to know.

The fact that Jenn was an anomaly made things even more complicated. Thirty-year-olds do not generally suffer massive bleeds in their brain. She was far too young to be in their NICU. I think when they looked at her, they saw their daughter, their younger sister, their granddaughter. Her youth made her illness more personal. And while I knew this would translate into the best care possible, the worry on their faces scared me.

When I entered Jenn's room, her eyes were closed, and countless tubes ran through her. She seemed so inaccessible, so small lying in her hospital bed. Her brown hair was tied back so the drain for her brain was uninhibited. I approached her, taking in her delicate features. She looked like she did when she was a baby, free of worry and tension, as if any disappointing or painful memories of her prior life were wiped away. My heart broke.

Tears welled in my eyes, but I choked down my sobs. *She might be able to hear me.* Gently kissing her forehead, I ran my fingers through her hair. Resting there for a moment, I inhaled like I did when she was a baby. Even with the wires and tubes and blood-matted hair, she still smelled like Jenn. I savored her scent. I desperately grasped this small piece of her—the only possible way to hold her essence close to me in the present moment.

My mind drifted to the old-time musicals we used to watch when she was a young girl. *The King and I, Oliver!, Oklahoma.* Both girls danced around the room to Rodgers and Hammerstein while I held down the words.

The music would tag along with us all day, and I often sang their favorites at bedtime. Jenn's was "Wouldn't It Be Loverly" from *My Fair Lady* because the lyrics included the word "chocolate," which was her favorite food. Unfortunately, every time she heard the word, she screamed and cried at the top of her lungs for chocolate.

As this was not the most effective sleep routine, I had to get creative. When the bedtime request came, "chocolate" was replaced with any manner of random words. When she got old enough to stop screaming for chocolate, she joined in on the improvisation. Singing together, we laughed as we yelled out nonsensical replacement lyrics, trying to best each other with the most bizarre word. What started as a parenting strategy became a delightful game.

A wave of sadness washed over me as I looked at my girl in bed now, wishing she could play our game. Brushing her hair back from her forehead, I sang to her once again of a warm, cozy room full of all the chocolate she could eat, how lovely that would be—and I thought of how she might reimagine those classic lyrics now.

I desperately needed her to hear me so she wouldn't feel so alone. Or maybe I sang so I wouldn't feel so alone. All I wanted was for her to scream for chocolate. I took her left hand and brought it up to my lips.

"I love you so much."

All the machines beeped in response.

The staff told us to go home and get some rest, but I didn't want to leave the hospital. What condition would Jenn be in the next day? Would she make it through the night? The thought of her passing away alone in her room in the NICU was agonizing. How could we leave her?

They promised to call if anything arose, noting our utter exhaustion. I trusted them.

As we walked out, I glanced at Mischa. Like all of us, he looked lost somewhere in his own head. His gait was slow and deliberate. His body seemed awash in grief and his eyes were constricted, red and tight. *What must he be feeling?*

He and Jenn were still unpacking their first apartment together. They were planning a life as partners. They had dreams. They were full of hope. Now everything was suddenly thrown up in the air. It was too soon to determine anything. No one had any idea where the pieces would land.

He cannot be by himself tonight. I didn't know how comfortable he felt coming home with us, as we had only known him for a short time. However, he was basically alone, since most of his family lived in Texas.

As we walked in silence through the main-floor lobby, I turned to Mischa and asked, "Do you want to come stay with us tonight or would you rather be alone?"

"I think I would prefer to come home with you, actually. Thank you."

After he went to the apartment to gather some clothes and his husky, Shadow, he set himself up in Jenn's room. It was so good to have another person with us who knew about Jenn, without having to be told, a fellow passenger on this unscripted, unsought journey through darkness. Someone who understood along with us that the ordinary can devolve in a moment. We were all now partners in grief, and Mischa's presence filled the quiet of Jenn's space with life and energy, almost keeping her alive for us.

David

The brain of a healthy thirty-year-old woman sits snugly within her hard, rigid skull. When something causes the brain to swell, known as edema, oxygenated blood is prevented from reaching the brain and fluids are restricted from leaving the brain. This causes the brain to compress, presenting a life-threatening emergency that can lead to permanent brain damage or death.

The first medical hurdle, therefore, was to stabilize the rising intracranial pressure in Jenny's brain. This is what the drain was for. Now that she was in the NICU, she was also hooked up to an intracranial pressure monitor that showed the amount of pressure in her brain in real time. The upper limit of normal intracranial pressure was 20 mm, so anything close was cause for concern.

It was late that night when my cell phone rang. We were so tense, everyone in the house heard it go off and came running into my bedroom. I picked up and put it on speaker. Fear coursed through my body. This could not be good.

"Dr. Goldman, this is Dr. Drew, resident in charge of the NICU. I'm calling about Jenn."

"Yes, you have our attention. Go ahead."

My response was clipped and efficient. We needed to know as soon as possible.

"Jenn's intracranial pressure is dangerously high. The drain that's in is clogged and we need to replace it. Do we have your permission?"

"Yes. In the future, do not waste time calling me. Do what you must to keep her alive."

I hung up the phone. My body was shaking, and my heart was racing. The rest of the family stared at me, clearly seeking guidance as to the severity of the situation. I had nothing positive to share with them. All I could do was to stay calm, keep everyone else calm, stay informed, and prepare for whatever lay ahead. My daughter's life was out of my control.

Caryn

The next day, I sat in Jenn's hospital room with my eyes glued to the intracranial pressure monitor, willing the number to dip far below 20 mm. The numbers on the screen stubbornly hovered around 18 to 19 mm. We were never far from what I began to think of as cranial meltdown.

The NICU staff came in and out of the room to check her vitals, read the monitors, and attempt to elicit a response from her.

"Hi, Jenn, can you give me a thumbs-up? How about two fingers? Nod your head if you can hear me," they said.

She was nonresponsive. I tried not to think about what this meant, although it was hard to ignore the concern on everyone's face.

Believe in Miracles Every Day was written on the drab green NICU family waiting room wall. I was panicky thinking about it. *Is this where we are? Do we need a miracle?* The overwhelming answer seemed to be "Yes."

The NICU staff described Jenn's condition to me as "critically critical." I brooded over what these words meant, and I was unable to shake them from my mind. What did it even mean and why were they saying that phrase? Were they trying to prepare me? Is it even possible to prepare? Would it make Jenn's ultimate death easier if I practiced her being dead in my mind? Would I be less grief-stricken? *No.*

Other families came and went, congregating in twos and threes, speaking with a quiet urgency as they discussed the prognosis of their loved one.

"How are we going to afford to keep the business afloat if Dad dies?"

"The apartment isn't big enough for an aide to stay with us."

"What are we going to do?"

I tried not to listen, but it was impossible not to hear their conversations, their pain. Everyone in this NICU was living their own nightmare. In some ways, I felt like an intruder, but we were also united. Thrown together by a common horrifying event.

I was doing everything I could to stay present, to keep my fear in check, to find some way to get through this. And with her medical condition yet to be determined, why should I obsess about the worst possible scenario? Wasn't it my right to think about it in the way I chose, to be present wholly and fully with her? Who owns hope anyway? I wasn't yet willing to give up my hope and faith. I was going for a miracle.

David

It was two days after Jenny's stroke. We had come back from the hospital, had dinner, and were getting ready to call it a night. Around 10 p.m., the phone rang. The NICU was calling again. My heart sank and I braced as I answered. Jenny's drain was clogged again, and her intracranial pressure was rising. It needed to be replaced urgently. *Not again.*

This was the third time. All I could think of was that each time they run a new tube to the center of her brain, they make a new path through viable brain tissue, essentially, damaging more brain tissue. I needed to go and assess the situation myself. Mischa came with me and we rushed over to the hospital.

"There really is no other option besides running a new drain at this time," the resident said in a detached, mechanical way.

We gave our consent and went into the family waiting room, which had become our home away from home. Within minutes, an announcement blared over the hospital loudspeaker.

"RESPIRATORY THERAPIST TO NICU."

Staff came running down the hall past the waiting room.

"ANESTHESIA TO NICU."

Mischa and I looked at each other. My heart dropped. *Is Jenny coding? Is she going into cardiac arrest?* I sprinted to her unit entrance. Everyone was running to Jenny's room.

I couldn't bear to watch. Even if I could, they would have sent me away. They didn't want me in there if my daughter was coding. Head down, feeling completely beaten, I returned to the waiting room. Mischa looked up at me from his chair and then looked down again. He appeared to be in a daze, staring at the floor.

Damn it. Damn it. We're losing her. My baby is dying.

My mind went into rationalization mode. Planning mode. Future mode. *Will I ever be a grandfather? Is it normal to wonder that right now?* I didn't know. My thoughts moved to Jenny. Her life. So short, but so full and so beautiful. It was over. Her funeral. Despairingly, I resigned myself to Jenny's fate.

Five minutes passed. We waited. The resident came into the waiting room. *Here we go.* But, he was smiling. *Wait, what's going on?*

"I have good news. Everything went well," he said.

"Are you kidding? What about the code?" I asked, my mind reeling.

"Oh, that was the room next to your daughter's."

"What?!" I screamed. "I thought it was over! Oh my God! *Oh my God!*"

My heart was pounding. I couldn't stop screaming. I felt like we had been standing against a wall in front of a firing squad, but they all fired blanks.

Once we were steadied, we said goodbye to Jenny and crawled home at 1 a.m., agreeing not to tell Caryn and Amanda. Everything was already too much, and this would just make it rougher for them.

We had just been pushed to the brink of death and then pulled back. I could breathe.

North Shore University Hospital Discharge Note, 8/20/21

Patient with clinical decline and worsening intracranial pressure issues requiring multiple replacements and flushing of the external ventricular drain. Repeat imaging demonstrates stability of the clot but worsening surrounding edema and brain compression. There was extra-ventricular drain malfunction and intracranial pressure crisis with bradycardia [slow heart rate] with short time need for pacing. Improved with mannitol.

Amanda

I needed Jenn to feel my presence even when I wasn't there, so I decided Bearie—the stuffed animal I'd slept beside since I was born—should stay with her. He has brown eyes, his once snowy white fur has faded to a dingy off-white, and he's lost some of his fluff over the years, but he's still a love bear. With him there, she would have my scent (an understatement). To sniff him and hold him is to feel me.

I outfitted Bearie in a pair of blue hospital scrubs, a scrub cap, and booties. When I explained to the NICU team how he could be helpful for my sister, the doctors and nurses immediately understood his role in trying to bring Jenn home. I was amazed at how they made him a part of the team right away.

They put him in bed next to Jenn each night. Bearie was close to her when I came to see her each morning. Sometimes she was holding him with her good hand. Sometimes he was on her chest, rising and falling with her breath. Bearie was there to make both of us feel better; Jenn being with him was Jenn being with me. I smiled, knowing she was calmer because he was with her. And so was I.

David

**August 21, 2021. Three days out from
her stroke. Jenny's birthday.**

This was normally such a happy day, but we were not celebrating this year. With her intracranial pressure still uncontrollably high, her medical team decided to perform an emergency decompressive hemicraniectomy—a surgical procedure in which a piece of her skull was removed—to give her brain the room to expand and thereby decrease the pressure.

The craniectomy was completed and with the brain open, a drain was reinserted into the optimal location. There were risks, of course: infection, leakage of cerebrospinal fluid, brain damage, extensive bleeding, and damage to the brain's vessels. But her medical need outweighed these risks.

As her intracranial pressure dropped to normal levels after a successful procedure, we began to breathe a little easier. We now had something to really celebrate on her birthday.

North Shore University Hospital Department of Radiology Exam, CT Brain, 8/21/21

The brain demonstrates interval left frontoparietal craniectomy. Unchanged 7 cm intraparenchymal hematoma within the left frontal lobe with extension into the lateral, third, and fourth ventricles. There is mild surrounding edema but no midline shift. Right frontal shunt catheter tip is seen within the body of the left lateral ventricle. Minimal hemorrhage is seen along the shunt catheter tract.

Caryn

David had prepared me for the fact that Jenn had a piece of her skull removed. What he hadn't prepared me for was how she would look when I would next see her. Splinted, casted, bandaged, intubated, IVs in both arms, eyes closed, looking emaciated and gaunt.

Her head had been completely shaved, which was jarring. For most of her life, Jenn had golden-brown wavy hair that hung loosely down her back. It was as much a part of her identity as her smile or her laugh, and it was jolting to see her without it. *She is going to be so upset when she wakes up and realizes her hair is gone.*

A paper sign taped to a piece of equipment directly behind her bed read *No Bone Flap on Left Side*. I wondered why a sign was needed and what potential issues could arise if a member of her medical team didn't know that a piece of her skull had been removed. I didn't ask. I didn't want to hear the answer.

In contrast, expressions of love flooded in from Jenn's coworkers on her birthday.

This is so shocking and deeply felt. Sending love, support, and prayers out to Jenn. You are a strong and beautiful beam of light that will get through this. Strength, love, and *prayers to everyone.*

We ARE more than a workplace, texted a colleague. *We are a family. And with all the love, support, positivity, prayer, and powers above, you will see this through with strength! XOXO.*

Not only do we miss your beautiful face, a sales associate sent, *we also miss your soft and relaxing voice during meditation time. You have no idea how much you are loved and missed. I hope all of your birthday wishes come true and that you will be back on your feet soon.*

May this special day remind you of how much you are loved by family and friends. You are blessed. Happy birthday! Get better, my friend, wished another.

Happy, happy birthday, Jenny. We know that you will be back with us again. You are so strong, and your positive energy and light will see you through. I am praying for you and waiting to celebrate your thirty-first birthday with you in the future, offered one of our managers.

Jenn had just turned thirty-one, and she was hanging on for life. I moved between terror and numbness as I tried to be there with her, holding her hand, telling her stories, whispering her words of encouragement, and singing her songs, especially "Wouldn't It Be Loverly."

Sleeping deeply, she gave no sign that she could feel my presence.

Amanda

Though I felt like we had been going through hell for weeks, Jenn turned thirty-one only three days after her stroke. Birthdays were always a big deal for our family. When we were young, our parents would decorate our rooms while we were asleep so we would wake up to a room filled with balloons, crepe paper streamers, and a bright sign wishing us *Happy Birthday!*

Jenn's surgery, the continuous flow of texts from coworkers and friends, and not knowing if she was going to live overwhelmed me. However, I still needed to make the day as special as possible for her, so she would know she wasn't alone. I directed my energy into designing a large birthday poster with photos of our dogs, the two of us, Jenn and Mischa, and our friends. Working on it distracted me from what was really going on and helped me shift my focus. I put my heart into it, thinking of it as a labor of love.

But when I brought the poster in to show her, everything hit me at once. A giant wave of sorrow knocked me off my feet, literally and figuratively. She wasn't there. She couldn't laugh at our little jokes. She wasn't going to share some ridiculous meme. She was barely alive.

For the next few days, I was too depressed to get out of bed. I slept because I was too anxious to be awake. My head throbbed; my back ached. I couldn't move. With this came crushing, tremendous guilt that I wasn't physically at the hospital to support

Jenn. My parents understood, but I still felt like a terrible person and a bad sister. My heart was breaking, but I just couldn't see her.

I felt dead inside. I couldn't get the image of Jenn out of my head. Hair shaved. A breathing tube stuck down her throat. Unresponsive. All of us standing there. All of us sitting around her. Not knowing.

Everyone's lives around us moved forward. But not ours. We were frozen.

I needed a break from this nonstop torture.

I texted my parents to ask them if we could take one night and *not* speak about any of this. Hospitals, nurses, MRIs, flowers, the smell of antiseptic. It was all too depressing for me to handle.

Maybe we can just watch My Cousin Vinny *and call it a night*, I wrote.

They understood and I was grateful. Guilty and grateful.

Caryn

Jenn's stroke had an enormous impact on everyone who knew her. So many people—some we hadn't heard from in years—reached out, asking what they could do. We were having a hard enough time trying to keep it together ourselves, and the truth was they couldn't do anything. While I understood people needed to feel they were helping, I began to avoid the calls and texts.

In some ways, it felt like a disturbing reversal of responsibility, like I was supposed to make them feel better. That was not our job, and, in fact, it felt burdensome. I knew there was no harm intended, but it all became too much.

There were moments I felt guilt alongside my anger. *Wouldn't*

I be doing the same thing in their shoes? Haven't I done the same thing in the past?

At some point, it occurred to me that if people could express their emotions around this event on their own, they wouldn't need me to help them. And so, when people reached out, I started to direct them to focus inward and look to the things they normally did to ground themselves and express their feelings. I told those who like painting to paint. I told those who loved writing to journal. Those who were religious to pray. Redirecting people to self-soothe made things a bit easier.

Some already knew what they had to do, and just did it. Our general manager got a tattoo on her arm that said *Resilience.* The twelve-year-old daughter of an employee painted an ethereal portrait of Jenn's brain in blues and purples. A friend sent us a continuous supply of delicious home-baked chocolate chip cookies. One of Amanda's friends sent us a beautiful note with a handmade needlepoint of a woman holding a bouquet of flowers. Flowers, fruit, desserts, and meals were regularly left on our doorstep.

A kind of grassroots community movement coalesced around Jenn. Everyone was either doing something to directly benefit us or doing something to heal themselves. It was all anyone could do with the weight of helplessness we all felt as we grappled with the realization that life is unpredictable, and it can cut us oh so deeply.

Amanda

Days passed. Jenn was still not opening her eyes. *I'm dying inside.*

Caryn

"Prepare for the fight of your life. We are at war, and we're not going to win every battle. We just have to keep marching ahead and stay focused on winning the war," said one of the attending physicians, suddenly stern, almost somber.

He was talking about Jenn's progress, and his words sent chills down my spine. *War? I'm scared of war. I'm not ready for battle. What battles can we afford to lose and at what risk? Are there any? How am I going to manage?*

As he walked away, I thought about the words doctors use and the power they have to shape each patient's narrative, as well as their loved ones' expectations and hopes. *Critically critical* was still stuck in my head. The word *excitement* was used to describe a serious medical event that happened one night. I was momentarily elated, thinking this meant positive news. Then I was advised that *excitement* is never a good thing in an intensive care unit. My heart sank as quickly as it rose.

It occurred to me that for these doctors to be able to do their jobs, they had to be detached not only from their emotions, but from the emotions of their patients. They had to stuff down their sadness, guilt, failure, lack of control, and loss. We wanted them to be completely in control, but the reality was otherwise. And I reflected on how amazing Dr. Woo was, to be able to comfort us through both his words and actions that he had Jenn's back and was determined to return her to health. From this moment of perspective, I not only forgave them and their sanitized words, but I also felt sad for the loss of intimacy and emotional connection that came with their necessary detachment. I couldn't imagine doing what they did day in and day out.

After just a few days, I was starting to struggle with numbness. I left the NICU at the end of each day and made my way to the fourth-floor elevators, which neighbor the hospital's labor and delivery unit. Each day new fathers were also on the elevator, their faces drunk with awe, carrying a car seat, sometimes with their newborn, sometimes without. Their eyes were shining with joy, pride, and optimism. I could practically see them dreaming about what their little baby might someday be. I could feel the love and the potential radiating from them and the tiny life they were about to take home.

Inevitably, my mind would wander to the day we brought Jenn home from the hospital. She was born with so much hair. Jet black and thick, it stuck out an inch from her head, setting off her soft, delicate features. In many ways, Jenn had returned to her baby-like state. If circumstances were different, I might have congratulated them or told them their baby was beautiful. But it was excruciating to acknowledge joy amid crippling grief.

There was something perverse about occupying the same small space as these new parents. My darkness diminished their light. I became numb and disconnected from my feelings because they were too hard to take in. There was nothing in my heart but profound sorrow and loneliness. I couldn't look anywhere but down at my feet.

Amanda

My mom tried to prepare me for how bad Jenn looked so that I wouldn't completely freak out when I saw her. I decided I was going to try to pretend that everything was normal and talk to her as if she hadn't had a stroke.

Even with the preparation, I could hardly keep it together at first. But I was determined to push through. I moved close to her, took her hand in mine, and started talking. I apologized that I hadn't been there for her the past few days and told her that she could count on me to be her voice. She didn't respond, but I knew she heard me. I could feel her presence stirring beneath the tubes and bandages.

David

Every single day of Jenny's first week in the NICU was a non-stop roller coaster. My emotional baseline was sadness and anxiety with peaks of sheer terror followed by elation. Then right back to sadness and anxiety, which had somehow become more pronounced.

Four days after the craniectomy, Jenny's intracranial pressure was stable but she was unresponsive. We didn't know if significant damage to her brain occurred before the procedure. Worried, the doctors decided to do an electroencephalography (EEG) to scan for brain activity.

This was an especially stressful, scary time for us all. It was a low point, and I lost it in the men's room. Mischa and Caryn paced the hallway and Amanda buried herself in her phone. It was an agonizing moment for us all.

Miraculously, just before the EEG results came back, Jenny spontaneously gave a thumbs-up to the nurses with her left hand. They were so excited they came running down to the family waiting room to tell us the good news. What a relief. I could breathe. Jenny's brain was processing information. We still didn't know what she would be able to understand in the long run, but this was a big first step.

Two days later, Jenny was extubated, and a tracheostomy (trach) tube was surgically placed in her neck to ensure that an airway was available should she continue to need it. Generally, a patient will be removed from intubation after ten to fourteen days to avoid medical complications such as pneumonia. A series of chest X-rays showed her lungs to be clear, her heart to be normal in size, and the trach in good position. All good news.

Amanda

My dad was a complete mess, and I knew it. He was trying to put up a good front and make us think he was doing great—the doctor who has everything under control—but I knew he was really struggling.

He couldn't stop sighing. Sighing is his thing when he's stressed. And with everything going on with Jenn, his big, long breaths started to freak me out. *Is there worse stuff going on with Jenn than he's telling us?* I needed to get him to stop. I was getting too nervous.

"You've got to stop sighing, Dad," I said one night as we all sat around the kitchen table.

"What? I'm not sighing."

I shook my head.

To show him how stressed he was, I created a chart titled "Dad's Sighing Count" and posted it in the kitchen. At dinner,

I'd show him how many times he'd sighed that day. There were certain days when his number of sighs almost filled the chart. And while he laughed it off, I was worried. It wasn't healthy, the way he kept it all bottled up inside. He had too much going on in his head. But I guess we all did.

It had been over a week, and I missed Jenn so much. Visiting was limited and even when we were there, she just wasn't. It was terrible being without her. I felt so sad that she was alone and disconnected. I needed to do something to keep her spirit with me.

I couldn't stop thinking about the nickname we had for Jenn when we were younger—Jennbug. In her almost childlike state, that name fit her once again. I wanted to get a tattoo of Jennbug. Just for me.

I decided it wouldn't be written in English. I alone wanted to know what it meant. I researched written languages and came upon Sanskrit, the oldest language and the language of the gods. I knew that Jenn had studied it extensively through her religion and philosophy courses. I loved the soft flow of the letters. This was the way to go.

I found a tattoo artist, and he drew a rendering of Jennbug in Sanskrit. It was beautiful. He inked my sister's name on the back of my leg. Small and subtle. Now Jenn would always be with me. I could feel her, and I couldn't wait for her to come back to me. I knew she'd think it was really cool.

Note from Our Store Manager

Yesterday was my first day back to work after being on vacation. There's a heaviness on all our hearts. We can all physically feel it. Jenn is on all our minds constantly. The good news we've been getting has been the highlight of our days.

I was so excited to let them all know that earlier today, Jenn opened her eyes and squeezed Caryn's hand.

If you step outside the store and look at it, you can practically see the love pouring out to Jenn and to you all. The impact her beautiful soul has on all of us is truly a testament to Jenn.

Caryn

I was feeling overwhelmed and lost without the structure my pre-stroke workday schedule provided. It was hard for me to leave the hospital because Jenn's medical condition changed frequently, and I wanted to stay close. Being there, though, willing her to wake up and recognize me—to give me a sign that she was still Jenn—was excruciating.

I felt disoriented and adrift. My life was on hold. Cranky and agitated, I needed to take a break, but I couldn't.

David

We were eleven days out. The swelling began to ease, but Jenny now faced neurogenic fevers because her autonomic nervous system was storming. The fevers—which were continuous and dangerously high—persisted for several days. They had the potential to cause lasting damage to her brain.

The staff put an ice blanket under her to try and regulate her body temperature. The blanket was set to such a low temperature that Jenny couldn't stop shivering, which caused her heart rate and blood pressure to rise. This was also not good. To counter this, the NICU staff covered her with warming blankets and prescribed Demerol to sedate her. She was effectively sandwiched between heat and freezing cold.

Caryn

As each new set of medical challenges arose and our little girl struggled for a future that had seemed an absolute certainty only days before, terror gripped us over and over. But was any of it a certainty? How do we live with the realization that nothing is certain?

I thought about her working in her small studio space in our basement, crafting blends of teas and oils. The scent of rose, lavender, and neroli wafted through the air, the sound of her voice rang out as she sang to some electronic vibrating beat, her favorite music when she was creating.

When each terrifying event passed and Jenn still hung on, only then did I let myself feel terror. Only then could I permit myself to feel the emotional battering I was taking. And when this happened, a profound sadness engulfed me, as did much bigger questions. *Why did this happen in the first place? How was this going to end? What was the lesson? Was there even a lesson? How does one be with the unknown and fill that space?*

I didn't know any of the answers.

David

Jenny's cranial pressure and body temperature were finally stabilized on the last day of August. Dr. Woo wanted to remove the malformation and restore the skull, stat. The cavernous malformation sat in the center of a large clot of blood. Using microsurgical resection, Dr. Woo removed both the clot and the cavernous malformation, which freed up space in Jenny's head and allowed her intercranial pressure to stabilize. The pathology report confirmed Dr. Woo's diagnosis. It was just a matter of time before we knew how her brain was impacted.

They got it, I texted family and friends. *They removed the malformation and the clot. The rest of her brain looks great. The surgeon says that it went as well as possible.*

The responses rolled in immediately.

Amazing.

Fantastic.

Best news ever.

God pulled her through. Our prayers have been answered.

We believe in Jenn.

And on and on.

I was relieved to finally have the diagnosis confirmed and the malformation removed, but I was already thinking about the next steps. It was just my nature.

Caryn

When I saw Jenn in the afternoon of Dr. Woo's operation, a line of large metal staples protruded from her hairless skull, holding together a gnarly bright red scar that ran three inches long. She had just emerged from battle.

The next ten days were brutal. Jenn was floating in some kind of netherworld, unaware of our presence. The most we would get would be an occasional smile and the raising of one or two fingers when we pressed her. We desperately looked for any sign of her natural feistiness, her quirky sense of humor, a raised eyebrow or eyeroll to express some irreverent sarcastic thought crossing her mind. It appeared nothing was crossing her mind.

The doctors and nurses were concerned.

We did not know what her new normal would be. The doctors did not volunteer information, and we were afraid to ask. Recovery from a brain injury is so individual, and the staff would speak only in vague generalities. They all did agree it would take lots of time, from eighteen months to three years. During this time, anything might happen. *This could stretch on for the next three years*, I thought, in shock all over again.

Jenn was like an ant crossing a football field in a windstorm, plodding along slowly but purposefully, trying to hang on and not get blown away. She was at the goalpost of the opposing team and had miles and miles to trek before returning to her own. There was little we could do to protect her or to hasten her journey.

How am I going to manage this? How is she?

All I could do was believe Dr. Woo's words—Jenn was young, her brain was neuroplastic, and she would make progress slowly over time.

Amanda

The huge, heavy-duty staples in Jenn's head were the first thing I saw when I came into her room after surgery. They made me sick to my stomach. I thought about how it must feel to have thick slices of metal in her head. I imagined her feeling alone and terrified, which was how I felt when I had my accident. I started to panic.

I tried to get into bed with her, but there were so many tubes I was scared I would pull out something major and kill her. The braces on her arms and legs made it impossible for me to hug her. I was sure she needed a hug. Tears sprung to my eyes.

The best I could do was to take her left hand—the hand that worked—and hold it in mine. I sat for hours just holding her hand, rubbing her cheek, kissing her forehead, and talking to her. I wasn't even sure if she heard me or understood what I was saying, but I talked anyway, forcing myself to believe that on some level she knew I was there, and she felt loved.

Caryn

For days following Jenn's stroke, the staff members at the store were inconsolable. Openly weeping, they desperately looked to us for signs of progress. It was complicated because we were looking for those same signs, but Jenn's prognosis was bleak and uncertain. It was so hard to hold space for them while trying to navigate our own emotions.

The general manager who had helped Jenn during the crisis was traumatized, as were several other staff members who had been present during her stroke. Jenn's screams were stuck in their heads and everyone was in an ongoing state of emotional turmoil. Now that Jenn was stabilized, we decided to conduct a group counseling intervention through our store's Employee Assistance Plan. The entire staff showed up, as did David, Amanda, Mischa, and me. It was surreal to hear their stories of what they witnessed that morning. We filled in the blanks for them about what followed.

I was surprised to learn many of the staff felt a strong sense of responsibility, as if they could have done more to help. It occurred to me, though, that they needed to feel they could have done more. This illusion of control helped eclipse the frightening reality of life's fragility.

"You saved her life," I told them. "Isn't that good enough?"

Amanda

Now that Jenn was on the road to recovery, I brought her some items that mattered to her. I wanted her room to be filled with the things that could connect her back to herself and her former life. I brought her meditation CDs and her collection of crystals and gemstones. Someone from work dropped off a copy of the Book of Psalms.

Before Jenn came to work at the store, she spent ten years building her company, Essential Rose, which sold essential oil products and teas she created in our basement. They were all amazing. I was so proud of how she created, manufactured, packaged, and marketed her products and sold them at farmer's markets and stores across the country. She had a loyal following, and her clientele grew every day.

Her Rose Gold Face Serum and her Sacred Presence Mist were her absolute favorites, so I began to apply them to her arms and neck. The room soon began to take on the sweet smell of neroli and rose. Jenn believed in the healing power of lavender, so I brought her a diffuser and filled it with lavender oil.

Hospital staffers came into her room and commented on the scent. Soon they were applying her oils themselves. They began to understand who Jenn was, and I thought this would translate into the best care possible.

I wondered if she could sense the presence of any of her things.

Caryn

In the hospital, we quickly learned to reframe our expectations surrounding Jenn's medical course. While we had originally hoped for signs of Jenn's improving medical condition, we soon realized remaining medically stable was the best news we could hope for. Non-regression was progression.

We were still teetering so close to the edge. It was unsettling.

Like the ocean tide returning to the shore, everything carried me back to Jenn no matter where I was. September was beginning, roses were blooming in our yard, and there she was.

Jenn's middle name is Rose, named for great-grandmother Nanny Rose, the elegant, powerful matriarch of the Hirshleifer family. Rose is also in her company name. And the regal, luxurious rose is her favorite scent. She used rose oil in many of her aromatherapy products, she added rosebuds to her teas and bath salts, and she included a smattering of rosebuds when she sent off shipments so her clients' packages would arrive suffused with the rich scent. White roses are her most treasured, she once told me, because "there is an impeccable purity to its appearance that makes it amazingly soft, elegant, and classic."

Jenn told me the bud of the rose is incredibly powerful because it symbolizes rebirth, new life, a second chance. I was left to reflect on her words, considering where we found ourselves. Were they prophetic—something to draw hope from? Or did they represent some perverse twist of fate? It was too soon to tell.

I thought about her Loving Kindness Tea, which she created in honor of one of my birthdays. Rose was the main ingredient, and she threw bluish-purplish rosebuds into the mix. She presented the tea in a small box along with a card she'd made using a muted green tissue-paper flower. Green is my favorite color. I imagined Amanda, our resident artist, helped her. I still had the note Jenn gave me that year—her words were too beautiful to discard.

When designing this tea for you, I immediately associated you with the qualities that lavender, rose, and chamomile possess. They nourish, soothe, and uplift. I realized these not only define who you are, but they encompass a greater theme of self-love and forgiveness you need to access within yourself. You are a light unto others and have a beautiful soul. I hope you can realize your strengths and begin to heal, one sip at a time. Love always, Jenn

I have words. I have no words.

David

Day by day, Jenny started to grow more alert, but the propofol and fentanyl kept her partly sedated. There were still times she did not respond to verbal and tactile cues. However, her eyes were open more often, and she was able to track a finger with her eyes and respond to simple questions using one finger or two. Plus, she was able to smile, which was amazing.

Machines were still regulating most of her bodily functions and with increasing frequency, her brain would storm—also known as paroxysmal sympathetic hyperactivity (PSH)—because her autonomic nervous system was reacting to the assault on it.

Jenny's storms came on without warning and lasted for up to forty-five minutes. Her blood pressure acutely increased, her breathing and heart rate accelerated, she sweat excessively, her body contorted. Her agitation would increase, as would her body temperature. Most troubling was what happened after each storm: When Jenny dropped from semi-conscious to near unconscious, she remained in that state for some time.

A storm is a diagnosis of exclusion. In other words, problems like infection or a significant heart or lung condition must be ruled out to determine whether a storm is even the problem. Because of this, each wave is a new cause for concern. We just had to take it day by day, storm by storm.

We began to talk about the next steps for Jenny. Before she could move into the next phase of her recovery—a sub-acute rehabilitation facility—she had to be off advanced life support (respirator and central lines) and her vital signs had to be stable.

Jenny maintained the pressure around her brain on her own for two days with her central spinal fluid drain clamped. They were going to be able to remove her drain. They discontinued the fentanyl and started giving her OxyContin as needed.

While her cognitive functions were still very much impaired, she was, after three weeks in the NICU, deemed ready to be transferred to the neurology floor. If she did well there, she would be able to move to a rehabilitation facility.

Caryn

Following Jenn's stroke, we were hit with an overwhelming outpouring of love. People told us about their experiences with Jenn, of how she had inspired them, taught them, and treated them with love and respect. Hearing everyone's stories and reading the notes from people she had touched were both beautiful and painful. How had she managed to have such an impact at her young age? Where did all her wisdom come from, and would she ever again be able to offer words of advice to a friend?

Prayers came our way in different languages and religions. There were so many wishes sent our way that David joked that if one more person prayed for Jenn, God would say, "Not Jenn Goldman again. Relax. I've got her."

The prayers came in different forms. On the day of her stroke, one of our employees reached out to her reverend who conducted a virtual prayer vigil for my sisters and other family members working that day. Some people believed if they prayed hard enough, God would heal Jenn. Some believed God didn't have that kind of power, and instead prayed we would be given strength to manage whatever happened. And still others believed Jenn's recovery ultimately didn't matter because whatever happened, it was God's plan and God would help us cope. A patchwork of theologies collaborated toward the goal of getting us through this crisis.

Though I attend services as often as I can, I didn't connect strongly with any of those theological belief systems, although I wish I did. I think it would have made things easier. The power of prayer can lift and carry you through. My strategy was to stay present and lock my mind into the here and now. I focused completely on being with Jenn, singing to her, telling her stories, putting my ear to her chest, and listening to her heartbeat. I told her about the very first time I heard that delicate flutter. I breathed every ounce of my life into her, willing her to wake up, to open her eyes, to smile, to recognize me, to send a kiss. It was our intimacy and connection that had the power to heal her, to heal all of us.

Wasn't that prayer?

A Letter to Our Staff

Hey everyone,

So many of you have been sending prayers and words of encouragement for Jenn, and we are so touched and feel truly supported by your love. It's been an emotionally challenging time for us, filled with uncertainty, and your wishes are so helpful as we move forward.

I know you are interested in finding out how she is doing, and what her journey forward will be like, and that's what I wanted to share in this email. Thankfully, the malformation in her brain was successfully removed. Both the bleeding and the swelling have been contained so right now, her brain is at rest.

It has to remain at rest to heal. This will be a long journey and we have to be patient and give her the time she needs. She is very young and healthy, and the neurosurgeons are optimistic about her ability to recover.

It is really hard to manage the uncertainty and to try to be patient while her brain heals. I pray for strength to be able to do that. I am also reminded that our power, as humans, lies not in our ability to control what happens but in our ability to respond to the things that happen to us. We have the power to be optimistic, take each day as it comes, and try to be grateful for the other gifts we have in life. Your support is one of those gifts.

Thank you for your heartfelt prayers and wishes.

—Caryn, David, Amanda, and Jenn

4

STEP-DOWN TO THE NEUROLOGY FLOOR

Caryn

Jenn was transferred to the neurology floor on September 8, 2021. When I was leaving the NICU, the nurse gave me a bag with the clothes Jenn wore on the day of her stroke—bright floral wide-leg pants, white sandals, and a white short-sleeve top. Her outfit was upbeat, light, and optimistic, like the potential of a cheerful summer day. But that day came crashing down only an hour after she dressed.

Her soiled pants were rolled up in a ball, her white top was cut into shreds, and strangely, one of her shoes was missing. It's hard to describe the power those clothes had over me as I took each piece out and held it. *What can they tell me? Where is her other shoe? In the back of the ambulance? Lost in the chaos of the ER? Why can't I stop thinking about where it is?*

I wondered what Jenn was thinking when she selected those pieces. What were her expectations of the day ahead? Did she have any premonition of what the day would hold?

Somehow, her clothes seemed to know what happened. She'd worn them, they stayed with her, they absorbed her fear and pain, they captured the day's terror and violence. I wished they could speak and tell me everything Jenn experienced. I needed to know, no matter how excruciating the details. I needed to be there with her as she experienced the horror. Maybe if they could, I would finally be able process this profoundly incomprehensible event.

David

I was so glad Jenny was finally out of the NICU, but I worried about her trajectory. Not alert or communicative, she spent much of the day with a low level of consciousness. She opened her eyes, awake for thirty-minute periods, but then drifted off for hours. Her head was deviated to the left side. She was incontinent and needed a catheter. She couldn't move any side of her body, although there was occasional movement of her left leg and left arm. I could see the muscles in her left leg had begun to tighten from non-use and her left foot started to drop. *We have to get her into rehab as soon as possible.*

Caryn

When the occupational therapist first arrived, Jenn was unable to keep her head straight or sit up on her own. I wasn't sure what Jenn would be able to do in this session, and I was scared to find out. A part of me wished I wasn't there because I knew it was going to be very upsetting.

The therapist brought a hairbrush, a toothbrush, and a few other items. First, she handed Jenn the toothbrush and asked her how she would use it. Jenn had no idea. She then asked Jenn about the hairbrush. Jenn seemed to recognize what it was, but she was unable to demonstrate its function.

At first, I was outraged and wanted to scream at the therapist. How dare she test my vulnerable child with tasks that obviously exceeded her current capabilities. She was in and out of consciousness with constant storming and sedation to regulate her temperature. It all felt like a sick joke. *What does she even know about who Jenn is as a person?* I fumed. What does *she know about the many gifts Jenn has?*

As I took in the extent of Jenn's state and considered the amount of work it would take her to return to pre-stroke functionality, I thought I was going to pass out. Was it even possible? If she couldn't remember how to brush her teeth, what did that say about her ability to write, speak, form meaningful relationships, and create a life worth living?

I started to think about Saturday morning minyan prayer service. I'd gone whenever I could for the longest time. I love it. At each service, the same prayers are spoken, chanted, or sung; sometimes I end up zoning out or reciting the words without thinking.

One prayer, Nisim B'chol Yom, acknowledges the daily miracles. The prayer talks about the miracle of opening one's eyes, sitting up, getting dressed, rising, touching the ground, walking, putting on shoes, and fastening one's belt.

Before Jenn's stroke, I ran through the words, not paying them any mind, taking all these little tasks for granted. After

Jenn's stroke, I was haunted by the fact that Jenn could no longer do every task the Nisim B'chol Yom mentions. It would truly be a miracle for Jenn to be able to do these things. I would never take these blessings for granted again.

Terror ran through me once again as I envisioned her beautiful young life lost. Too panicked to express my fears—since verbalizing only made them more real—I suffered in silence, isolated and alone with my thoughts.

Stressed and still baffled as to how we got here, I searched my heart for lessons, for something I could hold on to and take forward. If there was something, I knew it would be positive, not punitive. I needed something to be revealed, the emergence of a life-altering insight with the power to eclipse all the pain, frame my anguish, and elevate my understanding. *How can I best move forward?*

Amanda

Sitting next to Jenn in her room on the neurology floor, I drew a large heart on a sheet of paper.

"Can you point to the heart, Jenn?" I asked.

She pointed.

"Yes! That's awesome!"

She mouthed the words "Thanks" and "Amanda."

She returned kisses, gave a thumbs-up, and showed me one or two fingers when I asked. She even wrote a sentence on a piece of paper: *Mischa, you are a boy.*

She hadn't been this interactive since her stroke. I was really excited and proud of her.

North Shore University Hospital
Discharge Note, 9/13/21

Patient became febrile [fever] with temperature-max of 102. Infectious workup sent. No leukocytosis. Lungs clear. Urinalysis negative. CTA chest scan negative for pulmonary embolus. Fever is likely related to sympathetic storm [brain storm]. Cultures remain negative.

Caryn

The recurring theme for September was two steps forward and one step back. Moments before the ambulette was set to arrive to take Jenn from the neurology unit to rehab, she spiked a fever of 102 degrees.

In one moment, she went from being stable enough for discharge to requiring a comprehensive workup to rule out blood clots, pneumonia, infection, or worse. Even though we recognized it as a brain storm, the team on the neurology floor didn't know her, and they had to follow protocol.

It took three days to confirm her fever was due to a brain storm and clear her for discharge. It was another two days before a bed became available at rehab. These five days were agonizing. *What if another storm delays her transfer?* I worried. I just wanted something—anything—to go smoothly. I needed the curse to be lifted.

Thankfully, she was transferred after the fifth day.

Amanda

In the days we were waiting for Jenn to transfer to rehab, Jenn smiled at a joke her physical therapist made, she mouthed the word "yeah" when the therapist asked her a question, and she was able to hold her head up without any support when she did some sitting exercises at the side of her bed.

Jenn was a rock star.

Caryn

Though our lives felt like they were on hold, orders continued to come in for Jenn's Essential Rose products, and positive reviews continued to populate her online store. Before her stroke, Jenn had partnered with a commercial kitchen to blend and ship her products. This meant her business could continue and we were able to follow the orders, as well as see the reviews on her website.

Seeing the orders turned out to be agonizing. I knew how excited Jenn would be to hear about her business's growth and activity, but I also knew she was unable to understand any of it at this time. She didn't remember she had a business. She didn't know she created her products from a place deep within her and that they were a manifestation of herself.

Reading the customer reviews was just as challenging. One read:

> My friend gave me your Sacred Presence Mist last year and I'm obsessed. We are doing a holiday gift exchange with the theme "bring one of your favorite things," and that mist is one of my absolute favorite things. I can't seem to find it online, and I

was hoping that you could direct me. Thanks for making this product. Hope you are well.

I missed talking to her about her PR strategy, her cash flows and financials, her pitch deck, her nonprofit Inner Rose Foundation, and on and on. I thought about her brilliance, her energy, the fact that she never stopped thinking, planning, and executing. I looked to her for inspiration, for resilience, for grace. The fact it all was now missing felt like a knife slicing through my heart.

5

REHAB AT
GLEN COVE HOSPITAL

David

On Saturday, September 18, 2021, four weeks after Jenny's stroke, she was transferred to Glen Cove Hospital's brain injury unit for acute rehabilitation. The hospital had a great reputation, and we were excited to finally be moving ahead with her recovery. The road was going to be a long one.

She couldn't speak. Her cognition was seriously impaired. She was unable to visually track and had double vision. Her head leaned left; she couldn't obtain the midline or keep her head erect. She was unable to hold upright positions, including sitting, and she required assistance to move from sitting to lying in her bed, rolling over, or transferring out of her bed. She fatigued easily, and her muscles remained tense and activated when they should be relaxed, also called "tone." This is both a common side effect of brain bleeds and one of the hardest things to overcome. A significant amount of tone inhibited the movement of Jenny's right lower and upper extremities. She was incredibly weak and fifteen pounds underweight, as she hadn't consumed solid food for a month. She still had a feeding tube and a trach. Jenny had a serious amount of work ahead of her.

Glen Cove Hospital Speech-Language Pathology Initial Evaluation, 9/18/21

RECEPTIVE LANGUAGE FIM SCORE: COMPREHENSION 2 (out of 7)

AUDITORY COMPREHENSION

Body part identification: *within functional limits*

Right/left discrimination: *unable*

Sentence comprehension: *biographical, simple, inconsistent use of hand signs for yes/no responses*

Paragraph comprehension: *unable*

Summary: *Patient with moderate-severe deficits—able to follow multiple-step directions yet with comprehension breakdown at simple yes/no level; perseveration; poor tracking of objects; unable to identify objects.*

EXPRESSIVE LANGUAGE FIM SCORE: 1 (out of 7)

VERBAL EXPRESSION

Automatized sequences: *unable*

Word repetition: *unable*

Sentence repetition: *unable*

Responsive naming: unable

Visual confrontation naming: *unable*

Severe deficits—non-verbal non-vocal due to tracheostomy. Attempts to initiate limited but emerging ability to mouth words.

COGNITIVE-LINGUISTIC FIM SCORE: PROBLEM SOLVING 1 (out of 7), MEMORY 1 (out of 7)

Level of orientation: *alert—0 x 1*

Problem solving: *unable*

Abstract reasoning: *unable*

Visual perception: *unable—maximal difficulty*

Concentration: *sustained*

Memory: *long term, short term, working, immediate*

Summary: *Significant cognitive deficit. Right inattention neglect with left eye and head gaze reduced. Established eye contact. No tracking of objects. Withdrawn yet participating at times.*

Caryn

Rehab was the first chance I really had to process everything that had transpired during the past month. Before this, it was do or die. All my mental energy was focused on getting through the daily emergencies Jenn's condition presented. Every night when

I went to sleep, I breathed a sigh of relief that Jenn had survived another day. In this state of mind, it was impossible to process the many emotions I'd stuffed down. Now that Jenn was relatively stable, I could give myself the space to explore them.

I found all my emotions to be overwhelming and confusing. They were paradoxical in nature. I felt gratitude and anger, sadness and joy, despair and a deep sense of hope, profound loneliness, and intimate connection. It was so hard to hold it all while being there to support Jenn and the rest of the family.

The day after Jenn was admitted, we checked in with the physical medicine and rehab physician who was running Jenn's team. The only things she knew about Jenn were the contents of her medical chart, and it concerned me that the people charged with bringing Jenn back to life had no idea about the life they were tasked with restoring. She was voiceless and helpless to participate in her recovery at this time. Unlike all the other patients on the floor who could speak, Jenn was unable to guide the team.

I needed to tell them about Jenn, so I quickly wrote a short bio. Jenn's doctor promised to share it with the team.

About Jenn Goldman

We wanted to write to fill you in on our Jenn, who is currently without a voice and cannot do so on her own behalf. To all who know her, Jenn is a passionate, emotionally intuitive, inspirational young woman. She gets up each morning at 5:30 to meditate for an hour and she works out daily. At work, she helps manage a staff of employees older than her, and she does so with grace and wisdom. She is a reader, a writer, a thinker, an entrepreneur, and an awesome friend to many.

When Jenn was in her teens, she suffered from severe anxiety and depression, began to act out, and ultimately lost her way. We were forced to do an intervention when she was in eleventh grade, and she spent nine weeks in a wilderness program and eighteen months at a therapeutic boarding school. Through those experiences, she became extremely self-aware, grounded, and passionate about healing herself and others.

At Skidmore College, Jenn's fellow students saw in her a calmness, and sought her out for advice and for healing. She started a business, Skidpothecary, which she ran from her dorm room. Becoming extremely interested in essential oils, herbal remedies, yoga, Reiki, and meditation, she studied them all and used each of these elements to facilitate healing. And as she healed others, she continued to heal herself.

When she graduated, she began her work of healing others in earnest. She took formal courses in aromatherapy, got certified in three different types of yoga and in Reiki, took an eight-week mindfulness-based stress reduction course, and began to create and manufacture herbal teas and essential oils in our home basement. She would appear at farmer's markets and eventually was able to sell her products on Goop and Amazon, as well as at spas and other boutiques in NYC and throughout the country.

Working by herself seven days a week, creating and making products, designing labels and product information, doing her own social media, launching an online site, giving interviews, and eventually participating in public forums as well as serving as a motivational speaker, Jenn built her business from the ground up.

I have enclosed a YouTube link to several different interviews of her so you can see her at work firsthand. Tenacious, tireless, optimistic, and passionate, Jenn was able to overcome obstacles and reinvent herself over and over again. It is this inner strength we believe will serve her well as she navigates this physical and emotional setback.

Several months ago, Jenn made an important career decision. Unable to get the funding she needed to take her company to the next level, she decided to join my family business. We have a large, diverse staff, and Jenn's personal skills and unique outlook have made her a great asset.

We look forward to working with you all to get Jenn back to herself.

Amanda

My first visit to see Jenn at rehab was really hard. I was still so traumatized by her stroke, the fact that she was doing a little better didn't make it any less raw for me. I needed her back—her smile, her voice, her laugh, even her annoying habits that drove me crazy. There were certain things only we would find funny, like the quirkiness of a nurse or the inappropriateness of a hat in the gift shop emblazoned with *Living the Dream*. The fact that I couldn't share these things with Jenn made me feel so alone.

I missed her smart-alecky, hilarious, witty, mischievous personality the most. I decided to try and draw it out of her.

Because she couldn't speak, the nurses were always asking her to use one or two fingers to convey yes or no responses. I found this annoying, so I decided to shake things up by reminding her of her middle finger, which communicated more than just yes or no. I grabbed her left hand, pulled her middle finger up, and demonstrated. She gave me a devilish smile, and I knew she understood.

From that moment, she used it not just with me but with nurses, doctors, and therapists. My dad rolled his eyes and shook his head, but his smile told me he liked mixing things up a bit. Everyone else loved her sassiness too.

At least they were starting to see the real Jenn.

David

Jenny's rehab schedule included physical therapy, occupational therapy, and speech therapy for one hour each, five days a week. I didn't understand how Jenny was going to have the stamina to do this work. She became exhausted after barely ten minutes of activity when she was at North Shore Hospital.

I knew Jenny's recovery would be hard. The doctor heading up her team told Caryn and Amanda that Jenny didn't know she had a right side of her body. Rehabilitation meant bringing the right side of her body into her awareness.

She was still unable to speak because the trach in her throat prevented her vocal cords from vibrating to make sound. The trach also kept her from eating food by mouth, and it was very uncomfortable for her. Eager to have it removed or at least downsized as soon as possible, we awaited clearance from the otolaryngologist (ENT), as well as the pulmonologist.

Each day, Jenny's progress ebbed and flowed. One day she

would be waving to the nurses, smiling, kissing Mischa, and mouthing that she loved him. Jenny would identify the days of the week and months of the year. She would mouth the words to "Jack and Jill" and other nursery rhymes. Her nurse started to cry when she saw her mouth the words.

But then the next day she would storm. Feverish and uncomfortable, she'd drop into a nonresponsive, agitated state. Cooling blankets and ice would have to be applied. Her cognitive abilities would decline drastically. Even though we knew the storms would pass, they were still stressful.

From day to day, we didn't know what to expect. We'd arrive in the morning always hoping for progress but bracing for setbacks. Peaks and troughs were the name of the game. I tried to stay steady emotionally and trust we would make it through the torturous ride.

Glen Cove Hospital Progress Note, 9/22/21

Patient seen this morning. Overnight she was diaphoretic [feverish], but vitals were stable. This morning she communicated using thumbs-up/down for yes/no that she has some pain, possibly in the left knee, though her communication is inconsistent. Had right hand splint made by occupational therapist—spasticity in right upper extremity, particularly wrist, may be causing pain. Unable to fully obtain review of systems due to aphasia [language difficulty]. Pertinent positives include expressive-receptive language deficits, right hemiparesis, dysphagia, left knee pain, headache.

Caryn

When I gave Jenn a pep talk and told her how proud I was of the hard work she was doing in physical therapy, her face lit up. She mouthed what looked like two full sentences. I had no idea what she was saying, which was incredibly frustrating, but it was exciting to see her brain start to work.

When I got home from the hospital, I needed to be close to the pre-stroke Jenn, to touch her things, to spend time with that version of her. It was a strange concept—pre-stroke Jenn and post-stroke Jenn, but it was something I would have to get used to.

I started to go through the growing collection of materials I'd kept in her bedroom at home, and I came upon a Manifestation Vision Board she created, where she listed one hundred qualities she was seeking in a "life partner husband who is ready and open" for whom she would be a "forever match." The board was vintage Jenn. When she first told me that she was working on one, I told her I didn't believe in the act of manifesting things.

"Good Lord, Caryn, you're a child of the sixties. Get over your rigidity!" she ribbed in her snarkiest voice. I smiled at the memory.

As I looked at her vision board, some of her notes made me laugh out loud. In addition to listing the qualities one might expect in a loving partner such as generosity, charitableness, confidence, and the quality of being sensitive yet strong, she wrote the following:

Spiritual but not annoyingly so. Interested in consciousness, quantum physics, astrology, positive psychology, and believes there is something more but not in your face about it. Not preachy or dogmatic. Has a connection to New York and the American Southwest, Spain, Portugal, mountains, high desert landscapes, and cultures. Has a cowboy love of the land.

I had no idea where Spain and Portugal fit in. Of course, she also referenced finding someone who "is a positive astrological match in terms of planets and houses." I thought back to Jenn's phone call shortly after she met Mischa. She was so excited about him and about the fact that they were, in fact, a perfect astrological match. His moon was her rising sign, her moon was his sun sign, and his rising sign was the opposite of her sun sign. I didn't understand any of it, but I was excited for her.

When I came to the end of the board, my heart felt so heavy I had to lie down. I rolled onto my side in the fetal position. I thought about Past-Jenn I had birthed and Present-Jenn still waiting to emerge. Tears fell down my cheeks and left spots on the pillowcase.

Glen Cove Hospital Chart Note, 9/21/21

CT head scan ordered due to lethargy—showed no evidence of Cerebral Spinal Fluid leak. NSGY Dr. Woo consulted. CT shows very mild increase in calvarial edema, unconcerning. Neuro stable.

Mischa

The brain injury unit at Glen Cove rehab was a challenging place, to say the least. Jenn's stroke had left us all reeling in shock, and we clung to each other for support, processing the trauma as a family the best we could. But it was here, amid the endless corridors, beeping machines, and a variety of traumatized brains, that hope coalesced into progress.

Jenn is a fighter. She'd come a long way from the terrifying days in the NICU. At Glen Cove, she was regaining her strength both physically and mentally. She started communicating, feeding herself, and watching TV. She was working hard in her physical, occupational, and speech therapy programs. It was still early days in her recovery, though, and the journey ahead was still unclear.

I was filled with a mixture of frustration and awe. Overwhelmed by the uncertainty of her future, I couldn't help but marvel at the tenacity of Jenn's spirit and the resilience of her brain. Through it all, I clung to a sense of gratitude for her.

On one uncharacteristically quiet day on the floor, I suggested that Jenn and I take a stroll around the ward. She had recently been cleared to use a wheelchair, and I figured a change of scenery would be good for her. Jenn pondered for a moment and raised a single finger, signifying "Yes."

The nurses carefully transferred her into the wheelchair, and we set off on a cautious journey around the unit. I was still new to navigating the chair, and Jenn was in a fragile state. As we left her room, the nurses sternly reminded me not to leave the immediate area, as if I was going to whisk Jenn away from the exact place she needed to be.

We passed the nurses' station and were greeted by hoots and hollers from the staff. Jenn's face lit up with a radiant smile, and she reveled in the attention and encouragement. As we continued, Jenn observed some other patients sitting in the hallway. She looked at everyone with intense curiosity and compassion. I found myself aching to know her thoughts, wishing I could understand any part of her experience. This feeling had stuck with me since I first saw her awake after her stroke.

We circled the floor five times, and each time, Jenn eagerly agreed to another lap. Her head was mostly turned to the left, a result of the weakened muscles in her neck. I wanted her to have the full experience, so I suggested we change direction so she could see the other side of the hallway. Her enthusiastic finger signaled me to U-turn and push on.

We did another four or five laps in the opposite direction, and Jenn took in more of her surroundings. We peeked into rooms and stopped at informational posters. We explored some of the therapy rooms. I showed her the waiting areas I would sometimes escape to, and the elevator she would leave through one day, hopefully soon, on her way home.

She was visibly exhausted but happy. She probably would have agreed to keep going if I had asked, but we returned to her room and got her settled back into bed.

As I sat by Jenn, a warm certainty washed over me. For the first time since her stroke, I knew, without a doubt, that she would go on to live a fulfilling life. In that endless hospital hallway, amid the chaos and the uncertainty, I found the hope and courage to continue onward and face whatever came next. A potent blend of pain and love and fear and hope, unlike anything I had ever known, coursed through me as I held Jenn's hand and she drifted to sleep.

Amanda

On September 24, 2021, the doctors switched out Jenn's trach to a smaller one that would allow her to speak.

"Hello," she managed. Her voice was scratchy and weak, but it was the most incredible feeling to hear her say something after six weeks.

I burst into tears. We were all emotional. She told my mom and me she loved us. Even though the trach was smaller, it was still difficult for her to speak because it is hard to move air when something is in your throat. If you can't move air, you can't talk.

I had to know where her brain was, so I started to check what she remembered. I was excited she still knew the name of her friend Sophie's dog, Bamboo. She was even able to write *Bamboo* on a sheet of paper. Her writing was pretty incomprehensible, but I asked if she could write her name. She wrote: *Jenny*. She hadn't called herself that since sixth grade, when she became Jenn. I wondered how old she felt. The possible answer to that question terrified me, and I pushed it away, but it came back. In some of her other responses, she sounded like the thirty-one-year-old woman she was. It seemed like she was moving back and forth between ages and time zones. *How old does she think she is? Where is she in her mind? Who is she in her mind?*

Though it freaked me out, I didn't bother to ask if this was normal. I had come to learn that sometimes it's better not to know.

Caryn

The day Jenn spoke I was immediately overjoyed, excited, amazed, and so grateful. My heart was full. A sense of profound relief flooded my body—a seismic letting go—which made me realize the fear I'd been living with for six weeks. I thought I might never again hear her utter another word, sing, laugh, scream, or whisper in my ear.

Her voice was very weak and frail. It sounded like what I'd imagine a cat to sound like if it could speak. I didn't care. It was Jenn and she was speaking.

I thought about how much we take for granted. But I also knew how hard it was to live in a state of continuous presence, constantly recognizing and acknowledging the miracles in our lives. What is it about being human that makes this so hard?

A few days later, I made sure to arrive early so that Jenn wouldn't be alone. It was the weekend, and no therapies were scheduled. To be there just with Jenn on a quiet weekend morning was a profoundly spiritual experience.

As soon as I got there, I moved the chair up close to the left side of Jenn's bed, leaned in, and studied her quietly. The staff told us to sit on her right side to try and get her to turn her head in our direction, but she couldn't maintain that position, and I didn't want to frustrate her. Alert and engaged, she looked directly into my eyes. Our connection was powerful. I rubbed her scalp, its sweet smell staying on my hands and in my nose for the rest of the day.

We held hands, thumb wrestled, and colored. Sometimes we meditated together, using Tara Brach or Sharon Salzberg's loving-kindness meditation. She looked into my eyes as I told her stories about Grammy-oh and Papa Dan. I shared stories of David when he was a young boy and stories about her as a young girl.

My favorite was during a Little League softball game, when David, who was coaching third base, told her to go home when the person at bat had a big hit. Instead of running up the baseline, she ran off the field and started heading to the parking lot toward the car.

"Not that home!" he shouted.

I also sang "Wouldn't It Be Loverly" to her, looking closely at her face when I came to the word "chocolate," which I sang as loudly as I could, hoping she would give some sign of recognition, but there was none.

My heart felt like it was going to jump out of my chest.

David

I walked into Jenny's room to find out she had managed to pull out her trach tube on her own. She had a big smile on her face, clearly proud of her work. I was shocked but excited. I thought the trach had been in long enough and was holding her back. It must have felt great for Jenny to have finally taken control over something in her life.

The hospital staff were alarmed. Respiratory was called and tried to place the trach back, but they couldn't. Because Jenny appeared to be comfortable and breathing well, they decided to dress the trach site and closely monitor her oxygen saturation level overnight with a pulse oximeter.

Glen Cove Hospital Chart Note, 9/27/21

Patient self-decannulated and removed trach yesterday evening. Breathing comfortably on room air this a.m. Able to communicate using thumbs-up or down. Denies pain. Reports she slept, smiles when greeted by examiner. Waves goodbye.

Amanda

My head started to hurt so badly when Jenn was in rehab. Sometimes it felt like it was going to explode. The pain was sharp and constant, causing my entire head and neck to pulsate. Nothing helped. I iced it constantly, but the throbbing didn't stop. Sometimes I was nauseous from the pain, and some days I couldn't get out of bed.

When it was really awful, I couldn't visit Jenn at rehab, I couldn't pick up Luna, my Corgi pup, from day care, I couldn't pick up medication at the pharmacy, I couldn't do anything. I could only stay in bed all day, disoriented and depressed. I was the most depressed I had been since Jenn's stroke. I tried hard not to make a big deal about how I was feeling; there was too much other stuff going on.

Caryn

Jenn's face still revealed so much emotion. She was completely exposed, as if she was unable to access the psychological defense mechanisms she'd developed as a child to shield her from pain. When I mentioned things from her past that upset her, her face darkened the way a baby's face might, and tears ran down her cheeks like the wound was fresh. To look into her expressive eyes was to glimpse her heart with nothing to run interference.

Jenn couldn't give or receive hugs unless we got into bed with her and lifted her into our arms. When I did, she would use her left arm to rub my back, supporting me just as I supported her. My heart melted from the tenderness of her gesture.

It was strange to be with this softer Jenn, so innocent, accessible, grateful, ready to receive. There was a new purity to her, an openness, a simple honesty. It was an amazing gift to be with her in this raw state, but it also scared me to see my thirty-one-year-old daughter so exposed.

Will she be able to navigate life without defense mechanisms?

David

Jenny was starting to have a lot of anxiety about speaking. With her trach out, her speech therapist was focusing on getting her to vocalize, but the process exhausted and frustrated her. She often ended up gritting her teeth and becoming so agitated that her entire body shook.

There are mechanical aspects required to vocalize, such as proper breathing via exertion on the expiratory muscles. She was going to have to relearn these skills. She also needed the ability to organize and express her thoughts, fetching words and using her working memory. All these things were disrupted by her stroke.

Her speech therapist told me Jenny's anxiety about speaking would be the most difficult barrier for her to overcome after her stroke, and that anything we could do to calm Jenny and her anxiety would be helpful.

Caryn was trying to meditate with her every day.

Amanda

Jenn started to become really sad in rehab. When I visited, I got so sad for her. She was so vulnerable and exposed it hurt my heart. When I started to cry, it only made her sadder. Her face scrunched like a baby, and she sobbed along with me. Her emotions were right on the surface, and I couldn't turn away from them.

I tried to joke with her, tell her stories, share music, look at photos on Instagram, and spend time watching scenes from favorite movies like *The Birdcage*, *Dumb and Dumber*, *Napoleon Dynamite*, and *Best in Show*. I was scared to tell her she was currently paralyzed on the right side of her body because if someone told me that, I'd lose my mind. But it was hard not to know what she understood about what happened to her.

I loved to snuggle up right next to her in her hospital bed. She was so thin and frail but that didn't stop me. Sometimes we just slept. Sometimes we held hands. Sometimes I sang to her. And when I got home, I cried about her pain. I loved her so deeply. She was my best friend in the world.

Glen Cove Hospital Progress Note, 9/29/21

Patient depressed. Flat, less interactive today—spoke with patient's father regarding mood and medication options. Keppra can have psych/mood side effects. Will taper off Keppra and start Depakote. If mood symptoms continue to be an issue after adjusting seizure medication, will start Lexapro.

David

With Jenny's trach out, she was now ready to be reintroduced to solid foods, but she first had to pass a swallow test, which would confirm there was no impairment of the nerves that controlled her throat muscles. A stroke can lead to dysphagia—difficulty swallowing—which can cause choking and aspiration pneumonia.

To see if Jenny was ready for the test, her speech therapist gave her water to drink, applesauce, a graham cracker, and a fruit cup. Jenny did well.

Caryn

Six weeks out, Jenn had not yet regained control of her continence, although it seemed like she was getting closer. During a visit at the end of September, her speech therapist told me Jenn flagged her down in the hall and told her that she had to use the bathroom.

Excitement filled me. That was my girl.

Glen Cove Hospital Chart Note, 9/29/21

Patient was on tube feedings, passed swallow test today. Patient received a regular tray for lunch, ate 100 percent of meal, was able to drink water independently and making great progress in function.

Glen Cove Hospital Progress Note, 9/30/21

Patient will remain high risk for aspiration as vocal cords not fully closing based on ENT evaluation.

Amanda

We got big news right before the end of the month. Jenn passed her swallow test, which meant she could eat solid food. She ordered mac and cheese for dinner and was so excited. I was so happy for her, and relieved by her choice. Mac and cheese was her all-time favorite. Her order gave me hope that her brain was beginning to work again.

Caryn

I wanted to help Jenn begin to move through some of her sadness. The medical team told us depression was common following a stroke, especially with someone as young as Jenn, and the sooner we began to address it, the better the outcome would be. I had described the circumstances of Jenn's stroke to her in general terms, and she had listened without asking any questions. I knew there was more to be said for us both, and I looked for a chance to have the conversation.

One late afternoon, after Jenn's therapies had ended for the day, she was alone in her room, seated in her wheelchair. Mischa and Amanda had gone out to get her pizza. I pulled a chair up close to her and took her hand. She immediately began to cry.

"I think it's time we talked some more about your stroke and why you're here. Can we do that?"

Jenn looked at me and nodded her head, clearly ready for the conversation.

"So, something happened in your brain. Like an explosion. It was a bleed. Thankfully, the thing causing the bleed has been removed and it won't happen again. Your body, though, has been impacted by the explosion."

Tears ran down her face as she looked into my eyes. I didn't know if I could bear to continue, but I had to tell her. She had to know.

"Your brain doesn't recognize your right side, and you won't be able to walk or use your right side until it does. It can come back, but it's going to take a lot of hard work. Dr. Woo is confident and believes in you."

Jenn sobbed deeply as I spoke. It was awful to see her so sad, struggling to comprehend the magnitude of what had happened. I was wondering what she might be thinking and how she was trying to make sense of this whole nightmare. It was hard enough for me to process it, and my brain had not been compromised.

"This is a very emotional time for all of us. We all share feelings of anger, sadness, frustration, and confusion. It's okay to cry and feel all these feelings—actually, it's necessary for you to fully heal.

"Do you have any questions?" I asked when I finished.

She shook her head and opened her arms, inviting me in. I leaned toward her, wrapped my arms around her, and kissed the top of her head. We sat quietly, not saying anything for some time.

When dinner came, I cut up her meat, sat on her bed, and fed her. There was something so intimate about this act. But at the same time, it broke my heart all over again.

David

Jenny's physical and occupational therapy went slowly because she had too much tone in her muscles. Tone prevents the muscle from relaxing and doing its job.

Jenny's head faced to the left because of this issue. Even when we centered it with our hands, her head reverted to the left as soon as we took our hands away. The team started to use a neck strap to help her head maintain proper positioning and to prevent contracture. There was also too much tone in her right shoulder, right elbow, and right wrist muscles. To counter the muscle tone, Jenny began to receive Botox injections in her right elbow, her right forearm, and the right side of her neck beginning in October. Because of the toxicity, she could only get them every three months.

On the flip side, Jenny's memory was improving. She knew Caryn's birthday was coming up and Biden was president. She could remember specific dates and people from her past. Her sense of humor was intact, and she could understand most conversations. There were moments when she seemed to drift off, and moments when she took in what was said but responded only with simple answers.

She was still tiring so quickly.

Caryn

One day in early October, Jenn was quiet, lost in her head and not interested in engaging. I stayed a while and then went home, leaving her alone with Mischa. When he got home, he told me Jenn was feeling scared because things in her head were "jumbled and confused." She was upset because it was hard for her to think clearly.

I imagined for a moment the terror I'd feel if my ability to think or express myself were compromised. I ached for Jenn and planned to get to the hospital early the next day, set on helping her navigate this issue.

When I arrived early in Jenn's room, I sat down beside her, took her hand, kissed it, and then began to speak quietly. I told her what Mischa had shared with me, and Jenn began to sob. *My God. This is torture.*

Composing myself, I told her to think of her brain as a giant file cabinet that had been thrown up in the air. The folders and the papers scattered about her head, but her brain was in the early stages of reorganizing, and the process was going to take a long time.

Even as I worked to console her, painful questions ate at me. *What if she can't reorganize all the papers? Who will she be? What will she be left with?*

I forced myself to entertain the possibility that some of those pages may no longer be relevant or necessary. Maybe letting them go would be advantageous. Maybe some of the pathways in her brain were no longer needed and she could benefit from their being cleared. Certainly, mine could use pruning. Perhaps she would even find more efficient shortcuts on this journey.

Nobody knew what the fate of Jenn's brain would be. No one knew what remained, what was lost, what was possible to recover, and how long any of it might take. Burdened by questions that could not be answered, we were left to try to manage the uncertainty. *Will I be able to fill the space for her?*

Amanda

Every day I got off the elevator and walked down the hall into the brain injury unit, I noticed a framed poster on the wall. It was a quote from Ben Franklin: *Justice will not be served until those who are unaffected are as outraged as those who are.*

I loved the quote, but for the life of me, I didn't understand why it was hanging on the wall in the brain injury unit. Other than the usual hospital stuff and visiting rules, there was nothing else on the walls. As I passed it every day, I thought about who put it there and wondered when and why.

Caryn

Every day, I went either to the hospital or to work. Most days I bounced between the two. I was starting to feel lost and disorganized. I didn't feel grounded in either place. I wasn't sure if I would be able to keep it all together. I was sleepwalking through the days in detachment and disconnection. The sense of dissociation scared me. I couldn't connect with any of my feelings.

I thought of *The Other Love*, a Barbara Stanwyck movie I watched with my mother many years ago. In the film, Stanwyck has a nervous breakdown and is whisked off by two men in white coats to convalesce in a sanitorium in the Swiss Alps. I thought about how nice that might be to drop out of existence for a few days, to find a place where I could be free of worry and stress.

Yes, the Swiss Alps would be nice.

David

The severe recurrent spasms in Jenny's right leg started becoming a problem. She was prescribed anti-spasmodic medication, but the spasms still came on strong and without warning. The nurses applied heat and/or ice to the spasmed muscles. They gave her Tylenol. Sometimes the combination made the spasms subside. Often, I had to break the spasm by putting the weight of my entire body on her lower leg and bending it at the knee.

Sometimes, the spasms led her to storm, and we applied ice packs under her arms, along her torso, and on top of her head. The storming always set her back.

Caryn

October 5, 2021. My birthday.

When I got to Glen Cove, Amanda and Mischa were already there. Amanda helped Jenn make me a birthday drawing, and Jenn wrote on the card. It was in scribbles, which was sad but wonderful. The good with the bad, always the double-edged sword.

I'd spent time thinking about Jenn's old brain. It was literally gone forever. It died. The pathways, the connections—gone. The landscape was flooded out. Although some if not all of it would return, the brain that would reemerge would be different than the brain she had, the brain she was born with, and the brain I knew.

Maybe it would work more efficiently, quickly, or clearly. But it still felt like a tremendous loss to me. I grieved what was and what would never be again.

Amanda

Jenn moved the fingers of her right hand and her right arm the day after Mom's birthday. It happened spontaneously. I was there and it was crazy; I screamed at the top of my lungs. I was so excited by this show of progress. Her physical therapist, Evelyn, told me Jenn also had taken some steps during her session that day. Jenn had made so much progress over the past week. Her brain was starting to work again and thank God, her sassiness was coming back. Her speech therapist told us Jenn was still using her middle finger, which was causing a ruckus among the staff. They liked to stop by to see it for themselves.

When I asked Jenn about it, she told me she was just being "rebellious."

I loved that. She even called Mom "Caryn." I hadn't heard a good "Caryn" in a while. I missed it so much.

It was my responsibility to be there for Jenn, to make sure she was cared for and comfortable. I needed to make sure all the instructions from the therapists and doctors were being carried out by the staff. I could tell they thought I was annoying sometimes, but I didn't care.

Caryn

It was beginning to feel like David and I were inhabiting two different realities. He started sending texts to different groups of family and friends, updating them on Jenn's progress. The texts were so upbeat and optimistic they felt completely invalidating. They ignored how hard it was for us to get through the days.

The latest one was this:

Big week for Jenny. Started moving her weak hand/pushing herself in PT, OT, and speech even though it is frustrating/ the mental fog is lifting/more engaging when she wants to be/asking what happened/asking the doctor questions/feeding herself. We are very lucky.

Yes, there was a part of me that felt lucky, but there was a much bigger part that was just plain miserable.

One tough day, when Jenn was agitated from suffering from painful spasming in her right leg, he texted:

Hey, guys. Slow but steady progress. Jenny is working hard in her therapies and is starting to show some improvement. She's eating well, is now able to feed herself, and she is calling the nurse to use the bedpan. Day by day she's coming back to herself.

I was less upbeat. My perspective was aligned with shift notes from the hospital staff. For example:

More frequent storming over the past few days. Suspect anx-
iety/depression due to increased awareness of deficits. Patient
tends to get diaphoretic [sweating heavily] when changing or in
pain. Tends to get headache or knee pain. Right wrist has a resting hand split. Right elbow splint applied. Neck strap in place
for purposes of maintaining positioning, preventing contracture,
and relieving neck tightness. Intermittent junctional rhythm and
sinus tach. Awake, alert, following simple commands. Delayed
processing. Able to vocalize. Few word answers with some delay.

Also,

Patient crying on and off during shift as leg spasms continue,
compression devices placed, and passive range of motion performed on bilateral lower extremity.

I wondered how David and I could be experiencing such different things. I felt so alone.

David

Jenny was quiet and distracted one day when I arrived. It seemed
like something specific was upsetting her. I asked what was both-
ering her.

"Something's wrong with my eyes. It feels like I'm looking
through a box. I'm scared."

I put my fingers up and moved them side to side and then up and down and asked her if she could see them. She could only see directly in front of where she was facing. She was pretty upset, and I was worried, but I didn't want to let her know.

We knew her vision was impacted, but we weren't sure of the extent yet. We also weren't sure of the cause. Her optic nerve looked fine, and scans didn't reveal anything that might cause her vision to be as affected as it appeared to be.

I tried to reassure her.

"Yes, we know about your vision. We're going to figure it out," I ventured, but even I wasn't convinced.

"Why did this happen to me?" she sobbed.

Her crumpled face as she cried struck my heart with sadness. All I could do was sigh and hug her.

Amanda

Jenn told me she wanted to see photos on my phone. The photos of her. I got worried. There were so many scary photos from when she was in the ICU. I didn't want to upset her. She insisted, so I complied. She began to cry, then so did I.

I needed to be there for Jenn, and I felt guilty when I wasn't. Her pain scared me. It was difficult to witness. It was so hard for me to be there. I had just lost my friend Jake from a brain injury, which was still unbelievable, and now I was going through this with Jenn. In times like this, Jake was the one I would call, and he would always make me feel better.

It was impossible to understand where Jenn's pain ended and where mine began at this point. Was it my anger and sadness I felt? Or was it hers? Or was it both of ours? *Sometimes I feel like I'm a terrible sister.*

It was too much for me to process.

Caryn

Jenn's brain was finally beginning to wake up. One day, when I asked her how she was feeling, she said, "Good, all things considered." When I started to organize the cards and flowers in her room, she said, "Caryn, you just can't help yourself." When I asked her a question, she replied, "That's rhetorical, right?"

This return of her wit made me smile and reminded me she was still there. These periods of clarity, however, were punctuated by episodes of delayed cognition. Over the course of several days, I was not sure what degree of function or dysfunction I might encounter.

Some visits she was distracted, lethargic, and disengaged. We'd start to play a game of tic-tac-toe, and she didn't remember how to play. Then she couldn't remember how she met Mischa or that they were living together at the time of her stroke. I'd ask her something and hold my breath, praying she'd know the answer or at least that her reply would make sense. Sometimes it did, sometimes it didn't. When it didn't, I'd have to take deep breaths to slow my racing heart.

Jenn also couldn't remember any of her passwords. She'd lost track of her bank accounts, credit cards, cryptocurrency holdings, business orders, business contacts, IG followers—her entire life. It became my job to reassemble it all. As I worked through it, I was reminded of how unnatural it was for someone so young to lose her memory. Had she been older, her financial information would likely be organized and in one place. Others would know how to access it.

But she wasn't older.

Amanda

I once saw a TV special about a man who was struck by lightning. Before the injury, he had no interest in music and couldn't read, write, or play music. After the injury, however, he couldn't get music out of his head, and he started to learn piano. Eventually, he became a concert pianist and played the music he composed.

Jenn had come out of her stroke as some kind of music lyric savant. Not only did she remember the words to songs she used to listen to, but she knew the words to songs she'd heard only once. When we watched TV in her room, she could immediately sing a song as soon as she heard it on a commercial or a show. When I asked how she knew the words, she just smiled. It has been the strangest, most amazing thing.

Did Jenn's injury wake up something that was sleeping in her brain?

Caryn

Jenn started to ask me questions about what happened on the day of her stroke. She told me she had no memory of the day. She didn't recall driving to work, arriving there, feeling sick, or going to the hospital. She said she needed to hear it all, and I thought she was ready.

It was the second week of October. We were almost two full months from her stroke, and step-by-step, I took her through the treacherous day. I showed her an image of a normal brain and one of a brain with a cavernous malformation. Her eyes, momentarily afraid, opened wider. I couldn't tell if she was remembering or imagining how it must have felt. It hurt my heart to bring her pain, but there was no way around it. This was a necessary step in her healing journey.

As we spoke, it became clear that Jenn had no sense of how much time had passed—of how long ago she had had her stroke, of how long she had been in the hospital, of how much life had gone by. She thought five years had passed since she last worked at the store, and she burst into tears when I told her it had only been seven weeks. I couldn't believe how disoriented she was, and I trembled in fear as I thought about how terrifying it must be to completely lose track of time.

I had an idea. We needed to create a calendar for her so that I could try to orient her as to time. On a sheet of paper, I sketched out the months of July through October. I showed her when she had moved into her apartment in Glen Cove with Mischa, when the stroke occurred, when she was discharged from North Shore Hospital and came to Glen Cove Hospital, and when she was likely to be ready to come home. She simply couldn't believe that so little time had passed. I now understood why she felt untethered, frightened, and so confused.

I would get her a calendar we could use to record her daily progress and to look ahead. A sense of past, present, and future had to be created so she could begin to ground herself. The next

Hummingbird: the name Amanda gave to Jenn for her ability to defy expectations and chart her own path. A hummingbird can fly backwards.

Rose: Jenn's favorite flower, her middle name, her company name, and a main ingredient in many of her teas and oils. Like Jenn, the rose is fragrant, divine, pure, and quintessentially feminine.

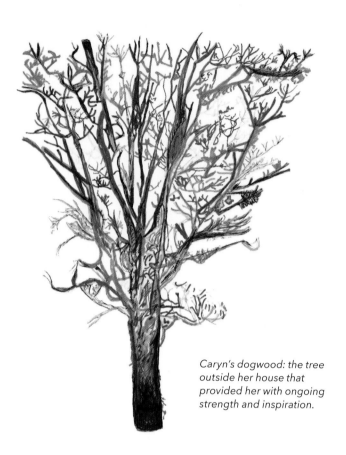

Caryn's dogwood: the tree outside her house that provided her with ongoing strength and inspiration.

JennBug: Jenn's nickname when she was young, written in Sanskrit and tattooed on the back of Amanda's leg.

Illustrations by Amanda Gwen Goldman

day I brought in a large dry-erase calendar and installed it in her room and wrote in the first box: *Day 1 of the rest of your life.*

Amanda

Jenn didn't remember how to use her iPhone, so Mischa got her an iPad, thinking it would be easier. She was catching on, but I couldn't believe how slowly it was going. Her issues with technology were starting to freak me out.

She couldn't remember how to FaceTime. Sometimes when I tried to FaceTime her at night, I had to call the nurse's station so they could go into her room and get her connected. She let the iPad drop onto her stomach in the middle of calls, so my view was her belly moving up and down. She couldn't seem to understand we're in different physical locations. When I showed her Luna, Jenn tried to pet her through the screen.

She needed to relearn so much. I couldn't imagine how long that was going to take.

Glen Cove Hospital Progress Note, 10/18/21

Occupational Therapy: *Sitting balance improving.*

Physical Therapy: *Ambulated 20 feet with parallel bars. Poor trunk control. Shows some initiation. Limited by right sided neglect, tone and weakness and right visual field deficit.*

Speech Therapy: *Moderate cognitive deficits. Using only verbal communication now. Improved initiation. Higher level cognition.*

Limited by impaired attention. Left intracerebral hemorrhage (stroke) increasing spasticity in right lower extremity limiting progress in therapy and causing pain.

Caryn

I wanted Jenn to speak to the neuropsychologist. She was resistant. She didn't know him, and she wouldn't know where to start. There was too much going on in her head.

She ultimately consented, but only after I agreed to set up a call with her former therapist, a woman she trusted and who made her feel safe. I made the appointment, so she proceeded to meet with the neuropsychologist. His findings were extremely upsetting.

Neuropsychological Assessment Summary

Patient presents with moderate cognitive deficits and major neurocognitive disorder due to cerebral vascular accident. Patient exhibits difficulties with concentration/working memory, delayed recall of verbal information (improving with logical-semantic cueing), visuospatial skills (visuomotor integration), and aspects of language (fluency, writing) and executive functions (i.e., organizational skills, initiation, abstract reasoning, and problem solving). Patient's affect is flat, and she denied currently experiencing any emotional symptoms. Her insight appears to be mildly impaired.

Treatment Plan: Individual supportive psychotherapy to monitor cognition, affect/mood and behavior. Continue with antidepressant and mood stabilizing medications. Cognitive remediation during speech therapy sessions is strongly recommended.

Amanda

The calendar Mom put in Jenn's room started to fill up. The first entry was on October 16th, when I brought Luna for a visit. On October 19th, someone wrote, *A Cranky Day*. Some days were marked *Chicken Fingers and Fries, Haagen Dazs Chocolate Ice Cream, Jenn's First Shower*, and *Lavender Mist Day*. Jenn's GI tube removal was marked on October 20th.

One day was labeled *Hydrating Facial Mask*. One day noted that Jenn went to the garden for speech therapy. She and Mischa put flowers in their hair. One day she became hysterical crying while painting a Halloween pumpkin. That one went over my head. One day she danced in her wheelchair in physical therapy. There were so many days.

And there was a new date on the calendar: November 4th. The day she would be coming home. I was excited. I was stressed. This would add another layer of emotion, and I didn't know how many feelings I could handle.

Caryn

Jenn's eyes revealed so much it took my breath away. Sometimes they were wide and clear. Sometimes they were mournful. They were always pure and open, offering me a way into her heart. There was an intimacy we shared when we were together, holding hands, sitting in silence. Sometimes, when we meditated, I opened my eyes to watch her. I could literally feel life pulsing through her body. It overwhelmed me.

These moments of pure connection left me feeling intensely alive. As hard as things had been, I saw them as a blessing—a gift to counterbalance the sorrow.

David

Jenny had an unexpected setback a week before she was supposed to be discharged from the hospital. She was using the bathroom when her blood pressure suddenly dropped, and she began to convulse. The aide with her called Code Blue. I was right outside her room when I heard the call and raced in. I found her sitting up, facing to the right, unconscious and seizing.

The rapid response team came running into Jenny's room. They inserted an IV, stabilized her, and determined she had experienced an episode of orthostatic hypotension, most likely due to extended bed rest in a prone position. This was the best possible diagnosis. If they had determined it was a seizure, it would have been likely due to the damaged area of her brain.

The staff laid her down on the bathroom floor. Though she quickly regained consciousness, she was a complete mess. She hadn't had an IV since she'd left the ICU, so suddenly having one must have terrified her. It was so hard to see her suffer. She was so scared.

"Oh God, oh God," Jenny sobbed over and over.

There was nothing I could do to help her.

As I stood there feeling helpless, the charge nurse recommended chocolate ice cream. Someone ran to the freezer and brought five small cups of chocolate Haagen-Dazs into Jenny's room. As soon as Jenny saw them, she started to relax. They knew her well.

When I told Caryn, she said Jenny's sense of forward momentum was undercut. Jenny was supposed to be discharged on November 4th. Was everything going to be delayed? It was traumatic and scary. Again.

For the few days following the episode, Jenny was highly agitated, crying often, noncommunicative, depressed, and scared. One night, she was so distraught we were called back to the hospital to calm her. Caryn sat with her, took Jenny's hand in hers, and sang the lullabies she sang to Jenny as a baby.

Caryn

I was falling apart. Everything was.

Amanda was sad and stressed. About Jenn being in the hospital. About Jenn coming home and what that might look like. About Luna barking. About not spending enough time with Jenn. About her own chronic pain. About everything.

I could feel a deep anger percolating in her, an anger precipitated by the loss of her sense of well-being and safety. She was angry that Jake died, that Jenn was so sick, and that she had to live with a sharp stabbing ache in her head, a stiff neck, and pain coursing through her body.

David was struggling too. His inability to problem-solve Jenn's medical condition left him vulnerable and on edge. He didn't have the bandwidth to tolerate Amanda's emotionality.

I found myself stuck between the two, trying to regulate them both while hoping I wouldn't completely melt down. Keeping David calm would keep Amanda calm, which would keep me calm. And keeping Amanda calm would keep David calm, which would keep me calm. What an impossible time.

With Jenn's discharge still set for November 4th, I couldn't stop worrying about how we were all going to handle this. *I can't take any more, but more keeps coming*, became my mantra. I seemed to absorb each punch. How much more could I absorb? What if I ran out of space?

I set up the call with Jenn's therapist, LP, for the last day of October. They would meet via FaceTime, and Jenn asked me to be there to help handle the logistics. She was still not able to reliably navigate technology.

I knew Jenn was stressed about the call. She was concerned about her ability to find the words she needed to express herself and keep track of the conversation. It took so much energy for her to remain focused for any lengthy period.

When the conversation began, I was overcome by the magnitude of what was going on. As Jenn engaged with her therapist, she gave LP unlimited access to her smoldering brain and allowed her to explore the wreckage and assess what remained. Jenn was defenseless and vulnerable, and she gave LP the key to search around.

The strength required of Jenn to open up under those circumstances astounded me. She was so brave. She was still able to trust. LP was so gentle, clearly recognizing the faith that Jenn had placed in her. Their session was profound and moving.

A Note from Jenn's Therapist, October 31, 2021

Hi Caryn,

I want to express my gratitude for having the chance to have the encounter with Jennifer. It was a profound experience for me as a therapist, a humanist, a spiritual practitioner, and mostly as a mother. Her innocent eyes and the smile when we had the eye connection was beyond words. It was a visceral experience of seeing each other . . . penetrating the soul of knowing the other in the presence of the quiet moments. She was seen and heard without the need for a lot of words. As I just said, she was in her right brain existence that she is trying to be and witness . . . and yes, her smile was at times mixed with deep sadness and tears.

Also, there were moments of her awareness of her situation that evoked fear of what life would be like for her . . . It's undeniable and understandable that she will experience profound fear and grief. She is entering a new chapter of her life that she was not the author of. It was not in her plan, she had no preparation nor understanding of. It was imposed on her, and now she has to figure it out and learn to accept and gradually integrate. Her innocent eyes were a testimony that her soul and heart are present and open.

It seems her right brain is intact. Her language and cognitive formulation of her left brain will need go through a rigorous healing process.

As a mother, I witnessed the most profound, reassuring, and heart-warming mother-daughter connection. You and Jenn have been in my meditation and prayers since the stroke. You are her true advocate, her voice, and her safe place.

All the best to you. ♥

Amanda

Jenn used the call button to call the nurse's station, meditated on her own, and FaceTimed with me. No technology issues at all.

Caryn

By November, Jenn was finally beginning to find her words and put them together in a way that made sense. I started to keep track of her progress because I knew that at some point, assuming her cognition improved, she would want to be able to share her story. She has always loved to hear and tell stories.

Her handwriting was still illegible, so when she spoke to me, I wrote down her words. It was amazing to see her brain begin to reconnect.

6

JENN'S FIRST ENTRIES

Jenn (as told to Caryn)

November 1, 2021

I am grateful that I am alive.

Mischa brought me a milkshake today.

That also made me grateful.

———

Amanda is my protector.

She knows what I need. She tells the nurses because sometimes they forget.

When she leaves at night, she makes sure I'm tucked in with Bearie next to me. She is amazing. I love her so much.

7

HOMECOMING

Amanda

When I read what Jenn told Mom, all I could think was that she was a superhero. How could she have no anger after everything she'd been through? For someone so young to have her life completely interrupted and still be optimistic and positive was beyond anything I could imagine.

Jenn was a child-woman to me. She had the wisdom and intelligence of a grown woman, but she seemed childlike because of her open, unjaded heart. It was like all the negative self-judgments and bad experiences from when she was young were gone and she was left with a beautiful, open, connected mind. Before her stroke, she had a protective gate around her heart. Somehow, this tragedy threw the gate wide open.

I had to be her protector and make sure nothing hurt her beautiful innocent heart.

Glen Cove Hospital Progress Note, 11/3/2021

Patient reported moving her right leg forward on her own for the first time during physical therapy. Also, she showed increased range of motion in her right hand, fingers, and in her arm/forearm.

David

Jenny was finally discharged from Glen Cove Hospital on November 4, 2021. The rehab team suggested she step down to a sub-acute rehab facility, but we decided it was time for her to come home. She had been in the hospital for eleven weeks, and we thought her cognition would improve more quickly if she was surrounded by family and familiar things.

We also decided to bring the therapy to her, and set her up with in-home physical, occupational, and speech therapy five days a week. This part of the arrangement was going to be temporary. Jenny was scheduled to start Transitions of Long Island, a highly regarded outpatient neurological rehab program on December 7th.

Lots of planning needed to happen to bring her home. We had to get her an electric hospital bed with side rails and a mattress, as well as a specialized wheelchair, walker, and commode. We had the bathtub removed and the bathroom retrofitted for a wheel-in shower. We arranged around-the-clock aides. Jenny was not sleeping through the night and needed assistance transferring from her bed to her wheelchair.

We had to find and schedule therapists. We had to set up doctors' appointments with an internist, her neurosurgeon, her rehabilitation doctor, a neuro-ophthalmologist, and a neurologist.

Busy was an understatement. Caryn did all the scheduling. I don't know how she had time to do anything else.

Amanda

So many emotions surrounded Jenn coming home. I was excited for her, and so glad I didn't have to go back to that hospital. If I never ever went back there, it would be too soon.

But I was also sad. So many nurses and therapists had grown to love Jenn during her seven weeks at rehab. I loved them all, too, for their kindness and care.

And then there was the anxiety around how Jenn would do at home and what the future held in terms of her progress. The pain of my stress had overtaken my head and neck, sharp and impossible to ignore.

David

I had the chance to read through Jenny's discharge notes the day after she got home. She had definitely made progress in the past few months, but she was still far from where she needed to be. Her Rankin score—a number measuring the degree of disability of stroke victims, with 0 being no symptoms and 6 being death—was a 4: *Moderately severe disability. Unable to own bodily needs without assistance and unable to walk unassisted.*

While this number wasn't a surprise, there was something truly upsetting about seeing it in black and white.

Jenn (as told to Caryn)

November 6, 2021

I have a new sense of purpose. I want to write a book. I want to share my story. I want to bring others hope and maybe help them overcome challenges. I see myself as a mindfulness teacher. I'm teaching a class with lots of people in it. I think of John Cabot Zinn: "Wherever you go, there you are."

When I get discouraged, I force myself to stay in the here and now. We don't know what the future will bring. I choose to stay present and let things unfold.

Amanda

I started to relax a little with Jenn being home. She was so positive.

One night after dinner, we were sitting together when suddenly she began to snap her fingers. Then, she burst into "Lovely Day" by Bill Withers. She sang in as loud a voice as she could possibly muster, completely joyful and uninhibited. Somehow, she knew every word. Her barely audible voice climbed several octaves as she lifted her hands to the ceiling and reveled in the truth of those classic lyrics: She was going to be all right. Mischa was by her side. Her whole family was right there, helping her heal.

Her spontaneity and joy were infectious, and it was impossible not to sing with her, so we did. We all danced around the room while Jenn kept time with her left foot. She swayed from side to side in her wheelchair.

After dinner, I thought about Jenn and a hummingbird

popped into my head. They're the tiniest birds in the world but they beat their wings faster than any other bird. They are agile and fast. They also symbolize joy, spontaneity, healing, and persistence. They do miraculous things other birds can't do, like fly backwards.

As Jenn's voice soared that night, she became our hummingbird. Joyful and persistent, she faced the unknown with strength and certainty. If there was anyone who would be able to fly backwards, it was Jenn.

David

We had an appointment with a highly regarded neuro-ophthalmologist just under a week after Jenny came home. We needed to address Jenny's loss of peripheral vision. He examined Jenny and conducted tests.

"There is significant peripheral constriction in both eyes," he informed us. "This indicates a certain right homonymous visual field defect with some peripheral constriction on the left as well."

He felt the hemorrhage within the ventricles and left frontal area led to swelling causing pressure on the visual relay pathways. The good news was he saw no damage to the visual pathways within her brain. Based on this, he saw potential for improvement over time as the ventricular hemorrhagic clots continued to dissolve and the pressure went down.

We would take it.

Caryn

Before we brought Jenn home, we were told that the next few months would be a big adjustment for us. Anxious because I didn't think I could manage any more adjustments, I knew Jenn would need twenty-four-hour care, and it needed to be the right people. Her aides needed to know how to take care of a formerly independent thirty-one-year-old.

Jenn was both a newborn and geriatric patient in one. She couldn't sleep through the night, she wasn't consistently continent of urine, she couldn't administer her own medications, she couldn't schedule her own doctors and therapist appointments, and she was completely dependent on us. And yet, she had the intelligence and worldview of a bright thirty-one-year-old woman. To see her inhabit such different life stages simultaneously left me reeling.

In addition to the people, we needed an unending supply of wipes, latex gloves, chucks, toilet paper, and paper towels. Oh, and we also needed food for seven adults—all of us and two aides. The washing machine and dishwasher never stopped. If I wasn't folding, I was loading. It felt like I was running a bed-and-breakfast at times.

The days were both stressful and rewarding as we watched Jenn reconnect with memories of her life, reabsorbing what had been temporarily lost. We celebrated Jenn in many ways— Japanese food from her favorite restaurant, roasted chicken (her favorite home-cooked meal), chocolate chip cookies, chocolate ice cream, and French toast. She went on outings with David, visited the boardwalk, and took rides in the car. By the time

Thanksgiving came around, then David's birthday, we had true cause to celebrate.

We were a family. We were in this together. We would survive this.

———

After a week and a half home, it was time to take a field trip. We decided to take Jenn to the store as a family—all five of us. She hadn't been back since her stroke.

Jenn was hesitant. She felt badly about her very short hair and the fact that she was in a wheelchair. She was worried about her ability to communicate and her tendency to become overwhelmed. She was anxious people would judge her. But ultimately, she agreed to go.

When we arrived, it was tough at first. Jenn didn't remember the physical layout of the store, the names of some of her coworkers, and some of the brands we carried. Without her peripheral vision, she had difficulty taking in everything around her, and she became tongue-tied as everyone came out to greet her. She was completely overwhelmed, and it was agonizing.

But after some time, she settled in. People were so excited to see her, even those who hadn't met her. They told her how much they missed her, how brave she was, and how she had touched them with her positivity and strength.

Some of the security guards congratulated her on her progress. Staff told her they'd been praying for her every single day. Some were moved to tears and told her she was a miracle. There were tears in Jenn's eyes as she let their outpouring of love wash over her. And there were tears of pride in mine. I was in awe of the impact Jenn had on the team. Emotional and beautiful.

The next day, Luis, the store's head of security, texted me: *It was so inspirational to see Jenn today, to listen to her voice and her words. I miss seeing her daily, and I know that those days will return soon.*

Jenn (as told to Caryn)

November 25, 2021

There is a family text group at work. I sent a text to the group wishing everyone a Happy Thanksgiving. It was my first text since August. Everyone was so excited to hear from me. It felt good to be back included in things.

I also received a call from one of my favorite nurses from rehab. I was the same age as her daughter, and we connected. She was amazed that I had come so far in such a short amount of time. I'm feeling good about my progress, and I hope it continues.

Caryn

By December, I was feeling completely overwhelmed. There was so much to take care of with Jenn alone—medications, equipment, home health-care aides, therapists coming to the house, doctors' visits, responding to the many people checking in and requesting progress updates, organizing meals, and doing laundry.

It all consumed me. Most of my texts to friends said something like: *Hey, sorry for not getting back the other day. Things*

*moving along. Jenn working hard. Coming back cognitively. Yay. Her
attitude's amazing. At same time, it is so hard. I have many moments
when I'm sad and pretty scared.*

It was so hard to keep up with anyone when I was drowning.

On top of everything, Amanda continued to struggle with
debilitating tension headaches and an overloaded limbic system,
the part of the brain that deals with emotion. When the limbic
system is activated, the other part—the cognitive or thinking
brain—can't function properly. A person's ability to tolerate dis-
comfort diminishes and they don't feel safe in their own body.
Amanda had seen lots of doctors, but a definitive way forward
eluded us.

We were all trying to manage our own stress and be there for
Jenn and each other. We were all struggling. Amanda would text
me multiple times a day sometimes, waxing and waning between
taking care of Jenn and her own pain:

> Jenn let me know that she's sad and having a bad day. Can you
> cuddle with her? It's so hard when she's sad.

> Jenn got frustrated about something and now she's really agi-
> tated. I hate it when she gets so agitated. I wish I could help
> her. I wish I could make it stop.

> My head hurts. So bad. Can you please bring me the two pil-
> lows you sleep with? Please. My head is not okay.

I felt so helpless.

Work offered some respite and gave me the chance to think
about other things. But from day to day, I never knew if I could

even get there. The sand kept shifting under my feet. As a person who needs structure to function, my stress was maxed out.

Jenn (as told to Caryn)
December 3, 2021

My mom told me one of my nurses from the NICU texted to check in. She is my age. I decided to send her a video. I told her how I was feeling, and I thanked her for taking such good care of me.

She texted me back, "You've made such a huge improvement. Everyone here is astounded by how amazing you look. We rarely see patients like you recover so miraculously."

It made me feel good and reminded me of how lucky I am.

David

I was excited for Jenny to start Transitions of Long Island on December 7th.

Jenny's physical therapy evaluation would be held on her first day; her speech and occupational therapy evaluations were set for her second day. Based upon their findings, they would put together an individualized program. The plan was for her to attend three days each week.

Transitions had a great reputation, and it was good that she would receive comprehensive services in one place. Also, she was going to leave the house on a regular basis, which would give her the chance to interact with more people and in the process, work on her cognitive skills.

We were going to be all right.

Caryn

I started to spend more time at work each day, hoping it could provide some structure and the chance to think about something other than Jenn. Work was still filled with Jenn. It was where she had her stroke; it was where I saw her lifted into the ambulance; it was the place I thought she'd never be able to return to.

No matter where I was in the store, staff and clients stopped me to talk about her, sometimes even pouring out their hearts about how much they miss her. It was so completely overwhelming I started to stay in my office when I was there.

I was too emotionally exhausted.

Jenn (as told to Caryn)

December 9, 2021

Today, I had my first visit with Dr. Woo, my neurosurgeon. It was a telehealth call. He hadn't seen me since I left North Shore Hospital on September 18th. Since I had been pretty out of it at that time, I never had the chance to speak to him or him to me.

The call was really emotional. My dad, my mom, Mischa, and Amanda were all listening in. My dad filled Dr. Woo in about my medical status and the pace of my recovery. Since I felt self-conscious about my ability to speak, I was quiet for most of it, listening and letting him take charge.

I knew I had to say something, though. I couldn't let the visit go by without thanking him for helping me and for being such an amazing doctor. As the call came to an end, I spoke up.

"It's Jenn, Dr. Woo. I have to thank you for saving my life. I wouldn't be here today if it weren't for you," I said in as loud and clear a voice as I could muster.

There was silence on the other end that stretched on for at least ten seconds. I thought about how much emotion he had to push away in order to do the type of work he did, and how my expression of thanks might have unleashed some of that. I couldn't not tell him, though.

Finally, in a quiet, shaky voice, he spoke.

"It's okay."

Nothing more. And then silence. I knew he was blown away.

Dr. Woo Patient Note, 12/10/2021

Jenn is now home from rehab, making remarkable improvements. She is able to breathe on her own and speak. Cognitively she has improved as well. Right eye has tunnel vision, but vision is 20/20. R side hemiparesis [unable to move on right side of body] persists but improved, right leg distal weak requiring a boot but proximal able to move. Right arm increased spasm and tone improving with Botox injections.

David

I joined Jenny at her physical therapy session a week into her time at Transitions. I was caught off guard by how hard she was on herself. At one point, her physical therapist asked her to sit on her knees and try to drop her butt down to the back of her legs. She couldn't get too far and suddenly she started to cry hysterically.

"I'm such a failure!" she screamed.

How could she think she's a failure with all she has persevered through? With all the progress she has made? It was the furthest thing from my mind, but it was front and center for her.

When we got home afterwards, I sat her down and said to her, "Jenny, I'm so proud of you. You are not a failure at all. How could you even think that with all you've accomplished and overcome? In my eyes, you are the greatest success story there ever was. I love you."

Amanda

My head felt like it was dying. I couldn't move. I texted Mom: *I NEED SOMETHING FOR MY HEAD. I NEED SOMETHING FOR MY FUCKING HEAD. CAN U PLS BRING ME SOMETHING FOR MY HEAD?*

I didn't know what else to do.

A Text Exchange Between Caryn and Jenn, December 25, 2021

CARYN: *Hey, beautiful. I have to ask you this. Are you trying to stay present or is that where you are without effort?*

JENN: *That is where I am without effort.*

CARYN: *Is it that you believe all will be okay or is it that you're not even getting to that place in your head?*

JENN: *I believe all will be great.*

CARYN: *What is that belief based on?*

JENN: *I'm being proven that.*

CARYN: *You mean you've already seen it happen and that gives you comfort that it will continue to be proven?*

JENN: *Yes.*

CARYN: *But that's faith, isn't it?*

JENN: *Yea I guess you could call it that.*

CARYN: *That's amazing. It's like people who believe that God's got them.*

JENN: *Yes. Well, I have SO MUCH to be grateful for. Like I just feel held by the universe.*

CARYN: *That is so extraordinary and beautiful and inspiring.*

JENN: *Like we're so blessed.*

CARYN: *Yes, we are. But you are living it while most people have to continue to remind themselves of it.*

JENN: *Yes. Because this whole thing forced me to slow down.*

CARYN: *But as you get back to working and your old life, how are you going to sustain it? How will this whole thing guide you or inform your approach?*

JENN: *It just will.*

Jenn

December 30, 2021

I'm feeling grateful to be alive. I'm grateful for my family and in love with life, with my progress. I am writing this on my own now. Every time I walk is a miracle. Every time I take a step is empowering. I have no complaints. Truly. I am happy. And at peace. And present. I realize how lucky we are.

December 31, 2021

Some words on Shadow, Mischa's huskie:

A whispering walk. Furry delight. A bushy tail that slinks through the night. A ghost. A presence. A shadow.

Some words on Mischa:

His love is constant, reliable, strong. Powerful enough to carve rivulets in mountainous rocky terrain, yet gentle. A peaceful warrior. A powerful king. A man, as he should be.

David

It's the new year. 2022.

Jenny had a visit with the rehabilitation doctor who was heading up her team. She told Jenny the tone in her right upper and lower extremities had improved significantly. She was also able to share that her shoulder still feels tight but there has been improvement with extending her arm.

The doctor administered the next round of Botox injections to Jenny's right upper and lower extremities. Progress.

Amanda

It was strange and funny having Jenn home in the state she was. With her brain not fully recovered, she often went through her phone contacts, possibly to see who brought up a memory. Next thing we knew, she was calling old friends, boyfriends, and random people from her past she hadn't spoken to in years. Many didn't even know she'd had a stroke. They would fill her in on their lives and then turn the questions back to her.

Without realizing her health status might completely freak them out, she would casually mention she hasn't done much because she had a stroke. Often, they reacted with loud surprise, and usually, they called me after to find out what happened. It was amazing to me how Jenn had no concept of how startling her news would be to others. We often didn't know who she was talking to or the role they played in her life.

One Sunday in January, a call came through on Jenn's phone. Jenn answered and put it on speakerphone since it was hard for her to hold the phone in her hand. To Mom's and my surprise, it was Jenn's go-to psychic from before her stroke. Unbelievably, Jenn managed to schedule a phone reading without telling any of us.

At first, we kept silent and listened to the psychic rattle off some questions about Jenn and her wedding plans. The psychic said she clearly saw the wedding venue as a winery in Eastern Long Island and began to describe details of the setting and the reception. She said she saw Jenn active and healthy, doing yoga, and working out.

"I think you're still running," she added.

We were dying. Jenn hadn't let the psychic know she had had a stroke, was in a wheelchair, and unable to walk, let alone run, before the reading. The psychic kept going, like a train rolling along, completely unaware the tracks around the bend had been pulled from the ground.

"Tell her, Jenn. You have to tell her about your stroke," my mom and I kept whispering to Jenn.

I wasn't a big believer in psychics, and I had started to feel squeamish about the trajectory of this conversation, although a part of me was excited to watch this play out.

Jenn just shushed us.

Finally, I grabbed the phone from Jenn.

"Excuse me. I hate to ruin your session but there's something you're just not seeing. Jenn had a stroke in August. She's in a wheelchair, she hasn't been doing yoga or running, and she's not been looking at wedding venues," I interrupted.

Silence. As the psychic realized she had been exposed, she tried to cover up.

"I don't know why there is such a block today in reading you. There's a resistance I've felt since we first started talking. It happens sometimes."

Resistance? That's funny, I thought.

"Yes, you are very blocked today and this doesn't seem to be working. Let me give you a refund for this session. I insist," she continued. "And I think it's best if we don't work together in the future. I hope you recover and wish you a good life."

Click. She ended the call. We couldn't stop laughing.

Caryn

We decided to return Jenn's leased car to the dealership toward the end of January. She certainly wasn't going to be driving it anytime soon. First, though, I had to clean it out. I was apprehensive. It held so many memories of Jenn's pre-stroke life, it was going to be like opening a raw, weeping wound.

Even though Jenn hadn't been in the car for months, the elegant, citrusy scent of neroli hit me as soon as I opened the door. Her Sacred Presence Mist sat in her cupholder. The rich floral scent always transported me to Queen Cleopatra's throne room. I could almost see her reclining on her seat as two male servants fanned her with oversize palm fronds.

A half-burnt stick of sage and some crystals sat in a compartment by the radio. A bottle of kombucha lay on the passenger seat. Her sandy beach bag sat on the back floor. I could still smell the sunscreen on the towels.

An overdue parking ticket was balled up on the floor. I smiled. It reminded me of the speeding ticket she got when driving through tribal lands in New Mexico. Screaming at the top of her lungs to the Navajo chants she was listening to with her windows open, her hair tussled by the wind, she was completely unaware that she was driving eighty-five miles per hour. That was my Jenn, joyful and free.

I missed Jenn's spontaneity and fearlessness. It had offered me the chance to vicariously step out of the rigid constraints I put on myself. Every time she got into the car and drove by herself to

Nashville, Detroit, Colorado, or wherever for a festival, I would experience her intrepidness as my own. And for the moment, I would be a free spirit too. It amazed me how she didn't need someone to go with her. She just did it. And I missed that.

She needed a different type of fearlessness now—the courage to confront the possibility of never walking again. Of not being able to use her right arm. Of never fully recovering. The stakes being what they were, this was a vicarious ride I was too scared to take.

I was embarrassed by my gutlessness.

Jenn

January 28, 2022

I am so glad that I have thoughts. They are not to the depth that I want. My brain feels sluggish and slow. Sometimes, I can't piece things together. Sometimes I feel like I don't have thoughts and that's scary. It's as if things are floating and I can't bridge them or loop them together or connect them.

I don't know how I know the stuff I know. I know about human nature but not in words. It's in feelings. It sucks but at the same time, I have this overwhelming feeling of gratitude and warmth and wholeness that fills my whole body for the life that I have.

The simple things like waking up and seeing the sunshine bring me joy. I'm so motivated to walk and exercise and do the things I used to do.

Caryn

Before bed one night, Jenn and I sat side by side on the couch, silently reflecting on the day. She seemed so content, and I told her so.

"I'm happy," she said.

"How?" I inquired.

"I'm completely present. Now, can you read me some Mary Oliver?"

I had started to read Mary Oliver's poetry to her each night before she went to bed. We both loved Oliver's elegant, insightful observations about nature and life. As I leafed through the pages looking for the perfect poem, I was transported back twenty-five years when I sat reading Jenn bedtime stories.

"Mom, please read me a story," she would ask. I always jumped at the chance to share the magic of books with her.

To have the occasion to read a poem or bedtime story to my thirty-one-year-old daughter was both rare and exquisite. It was a chance to give to her in a way I hadn't been able to since she was young. It was a chance to connect with her open, loving, undefended tender heart in return.

As we sat reading together, I looked into her expressive eyes, which revealed her depth and beauty. Her smile was soft, loving, inviting. There was nothing she held back. We took one another's hands. It felt so natural as tears splashed on our cheeks.

What an extraordinarily intimate and precious time in our lives.

Jenn

February 3, 2022

My day today was amazing because I walked. Walking makes me feel empowered, like I'm taking my life back. It's tangible. I can see the progress. I've been walking these past few weeks, but only by literally leaning on someone else for support. The rest of the time, I'm in my wheelchair. Today, I went to physical therapy and when we walked, the therapist used as little support as possible to help me. It was just her hand placed on my shoulder and the rest was me. I was so proud.

Three days a week, I go to Transitions for physical, occupational, and speech therapy. It's hard because I'm constantly pushed to my limits. I'm also pushing myself to my limits. I am very motivated to heal. I want to be able to exercise again, to do yoga, to meditate with my back straight, to walk through the woods, to climb a mountain, to dance.

I have no bitterness around the fact that this happened to me. The fact that I survived makes me joyful. I just feel gratitude. I feel like I've been chosen to share my story.

Caryn

I was sitting at the dining room table and heard sounds coming from Jenn's room. *She must be up from her nap*, I thought. I looked toward her room, expecting to see her turn the corner and head down the hallway. And then I remembered she couldn't walk. It was a crushing blow every time.

Jenn

February 5, 2022

You become what you most often think about. What we put our attention on grows. That's why I changed the screen saver on my phone from an image of water to a screenshot of one of my daily affirmations: *Good things are coming my way.* This is the mindset I want to embody.

My mother was amazed at how I could be so positive even after everything that's happened. To me, it's empowering to put what I want out into the universe where it can be heard. There are other affirmations I also repeat to myself. *I am well. I have strength. I am getting better every day.* This might not be present for me yet, but speaking as if it is brings it into my reach. I can see myself in a place of power and strength, and that inspires me to continue to work hard.

February 15, 2022

I feel positive today. I woke up and had a nice conversation with my uncle. I still fear the inexplicable pause when I am speaking. It feels like all the pressure is on me and I'm being squeezed from the inside out. Even though we're all entitled to lose our train of thought from time to time, I can't let myself off the hook when it happens to me.

Yesterday, I called in to a meeting at the store for the first time since my stroke. I forgot the point I was trying to make, and I panicked. Scrambling to find the words, I felt like I was struggling to hold on. I took a deep breath and regained my sense of control. And the words came to me. I was relieved I could attend the meeting over the phone. The pandemic made that all the more normal.

But for me, it's not just my worrying about my speaking. There's also the fact that my hair is so short, I can't walk, and I'm feeling very insecure about my physical appearance. I don't want to go to work until I feel like I can be my best self when I'm there. My mom tells me that I'm perfect the way I am, but my mom always says that.

8

SEIZURES

Jenn

February 16, 2022

Amanda had a grand mal seizure right in front of me and my mom last night. I was sitting at the table with my mom when suddenly Amanda's body stiffened, her arms shot out in front of her, her eyes became hyper-focused as she stared straight ahead, and she started walking backwards. It looked like she was in some kind of trance. We screamed and then she fell backwards onto the wooden floor, hitting her skull on the ground. Blood began to pool under her head as she convulsed. I didn't know what was happening to her, but my dad was in the next room and saw the end of the episode.

We called 911 and an ambulance arrived. The EMTs bandaged her head, inserted an IV, and took her out of the house on a stretcher. She was headed to North Shore Hospital, the same hospital I had been at for my stroke. My mom and dad followed behind in their car.

Images of Amanda seizing kept flashing through my mind. It was really violent and scary. Her pale face, her wide eyes, her trance-like walk backwards, and a pool of bright blood growing around her head. She uttered nonsensical chatter before she went down, like she was speaking in tongues. I thought about what my mother must have felt, hearing Amanda and being reminded of what I had sounded like when I had my stroke.

I couldn't stop thinking about what it would be like to lose her. She's my pride and joy, my sunshine, she took care of me when I couldn't take care of myself. She spoke for me when I couldn't speak for myself. I owe her everything.

An Email to the Family, February 18, 2022

Hey Guys,

Thought it was easiest to write you all to explain what is going on with Jenn and Amanda.

Jenn saw her neurosurgeon yesterday. He had seen her MRI that was done two weeks ago, and he was very pleased. He said her brain looks clean except for the scarring where the bleed was. Cognitively, she's doing very well, and he does expect her to get her mobility back. From his mouth to God's ears.

The one issue is her vision. She has no peripheral vision but also, her vision is box-like so she can't see up or down unless she moves her head up or down. He doesn't see a medical reason on her MRI to explain this. He recommended that we consult with a second neuro-ophthalmologist, and we will do that.

The tissue mass to the left of her eye is muscle that was pulled down during the brain surgery. He can repair it, but it would require him to go back into her skull and lift it. A plastic surgeon might be able to do something less invasive, but that is not a major focus right now. Jenn is upset about her vision but she's still full of gratitude.

And I know it sounds crazy, but Amanda had a full-blown grand mal seizure on Tuesday night right in front of Jenn and me. They don't call it that anymore, but whatever. During the seizure, she fell back and smashed her head on the floor. When she got to the ER, they stitched her head and sent her to a room on the fourth floor, close to the room Jenn had stayed in (unsettling). It was traumatizing to hear the calls of "Code Stroke Emergency Room" over the loudspeaker. It took me right back to August 18th.

The tests as to why this happened were inconclusive. She did have an MRI, but we are waiting for the results. That will conclusively tell us if there are any lesions in her brain and rule out a cavernous malformation, the vascular malformation that caused Jenn's stroke. I'm hoping that the MRI might also give us a handle on why she's been having such bad headaches. If the MRI is negative, we must keep looking to find out why she seized, knowing another seizure can happen at any time, or it can never happen again. We plan to take her to a seizure specialist and go from there.

So, the update is that we don't know why this happened, it can happen again anytime, or it can never happen again. Last, she is not permitted to drive for one year. That's completely devastating for her.

That's where things presently are. As I learn more, I will let you all know.

—Caryn

Jenn

February 20, 2022

It was late afternoon on February 18th. Amanda came home from the hospital earlier in the day. At 5:30, she left with my parents to see a seizure specialist who agreed to squeeze her in. I was home with Mischa watching TV. We had just ordered food on DoorDash, and I was relaxing on the couch.

The next thing I knew, I was in an ambulance with Mischa and two other EMTs. One was driving and the other was in the back with me. I remember hearing the siren and seeing the flashing lights. I was disoriented, which made me panicky. I had a terrible headache. I hadn't had one since the cavernous malformation was removed.

The EMTs told me I'd had a seizure, and it was probably related to my stroke. It was literally six months to the day I'd had my stroke. What odd timing. After stabilizing me and getting a CAT scan, the doctors sent me to a room on the fourth floor across the hall from the room I stayed in just a few months ago when they stepped me down from the ICU.

While this fact was weird for me, the strangest part was Amanda had been just a few doors down only three days earlier. Even crazier, one of my favorite nurses had been Amanda's nurse, and Amanda had filled her in on my progress. Three days later, I appeared and was placed under her care. She was amazed that I could now talk, sit up, and breathe on my own.

The doctors concluded my seizure was from scar tissue that had formed in my brain after my stroke, something pretty common after a brain bleed. They put me on anti-seizure medication and sent me home. I hope the medication can control the seizures because they're terrifying. I could hear people trying to help me and reach out to me, but I just was not able to respond. Words couldn't come out, nothing made sense. I felt completely confused, disoriented, and totally out of control.

Amanda

I drafted an email to my mom to express how upset I felt around all that had happened.

Reasons I am very upset:

My seizure traumatized me.

I hate hospitals. They make me feel very out of control.

The doctor didn't see me as a person or care what I was telling her. She was mean and heartless and made me feel like an object.

The IV was put in in a bad place. It pulled at my skin and the hair on my arm.

I was on the same floor as Jenn was when she had her stroke, and I couldn't stop thinking about it.

Some of the nurses who cared for her when she had her stroke took care of me.

Some of the nurses who cared for her when she had her stroke and who took care of me for my seizure took care of her for her seizure.

Her stroke was traumatic for me.

Her seizure was traumatic for me.

I feel bad she had to return to the same ER she was in six months before.

Jenn handled her seizure better than I handled mine. Why can't I be as strong as she is?

This is too much for Mom and she has no more energy to give. I feel guilty she has to deal with all of this.

I'm too upset to work and that makes me feel like a failure.

I'm not allowed to drive for one year. At all. I have no control.

Caryn

Seizure the day.

Not to be macabre but that's where I was by March. Double the neurology appointments, double the EEGs and brain scans, double the anti-seizure medications, double the terror of further episodes, hospitalizations, and setbacks that follow.

The brain fog that followed seizures was the scariest part for me—especially with Jenn, who was struggling to regain her full cognition. Reason told me all will be regained, but each upset triggered an avalanche of fear and left me without reason.

The seizure specialist told me that in his thirty-five-year history of practicing medicine, he had never seen two sisters experience first-time grand mal seizures within three days of each other.

Why us, I thought. *Make it all stop!*

9

ONE DAY AT A TIME

Jenn

March 7, 2022

I tell myself to stay present. Presence is the gateway to hope. When I think about the future, I get sad, like I was feeling today. I think about *What ifs. What if I don't get better? What if I can never walk again? What if my right side is always messed up?* I believe I am going to regain my walking and the use of my right side, but I sometimes doubt it.

The work I'm doing is extremely hard. I have to relearn everything and teach my body and mind how to be in the world—how to think, how to hold different ideas at the same time so that I can speak with intelligence, how to modulate my voice so I can be heard and have my words connect me with others.

I see progress, like when I do a good job walking, and that makes me feel really good and proud. When I learn a technique with my voice to make it louder, that makes me feel really good. When I'm able to write sentences like the ones I'm writing here, I feel accomplished.

I notice the people around me at Transitions and I see their progress. Most people are older than me and are not in a wheel-chair. They use walkers or canes. They are more mobile than me. Depending on the day, it can make me feel bad or be motivating.

I feel brave because I'm taking on my challenges, one day at a time and one step at a time. And I've been supported by the love of my family and Mischa.

Caryn

My deep need for connection led me to create a space of safety, acceptance, and love for us to return to at the end of each day. I have always filled the house with flowers, candles, favorite foods, and set out a jigsaw puzzle on the table. I cook as often as possible, but whether we order in or eat my home-cooked meal, we sit together as a family. Some nights we eat in complete silence, too weary and too terrified to speak. Some nights, we tell stories and even laugh. We reflect on how hard it is to do basic taken-for-granted-tasks such as sitting up, standing, walking.

As much as I tried to be present, I was feeling very depressed and disconnected. Friends and family offered their support and showed me their love, but I still felt the sense that I was walking this alone. I was in a dark room with no windows, so black I couldn't see anything. While I heard others outside the room encouraging me, I knew only I could figure out how to find the door.

Going to sleep was always the hardest time of the day. I felt most alone with my fears and sadness at night. Waking up was only slightly better, as I was immediately flooded with fear and uncertainty. *What will today bring?* I worry.

Perhaps, it will prove to be a day of progress.

Grieving is such a singular process because it is a product of what you carry as a unique individual, your worldview, and the experiences that have shaped you. Even among David, Amanda, Mischa, Jenn, and myself, we were coming through grief in our own way. And that felt so lonely.

Jenn

March 7, 2022

I asked my mom to set up some extra physical therapy sessions.

"I can't walk, and I really fucking want to," I told her. "I want to walk, drive, and exercise again."

"I want those things for you too, Jenn."

"I know you do. And it makes me feel bad because it feels like I am disappointing you by not being able to do them now."

"I want them because you want them. And you are doing amazingly well. Honestly. You're my hero. You can never disappoint me."

March 15, 2022

I had a follow-up visit with my neuro-ophthalmologist today. Since the stroke, I have been essentially blind in my periphery on both sides, and I can't really see above or below where my eyes are focused. It's terrifying to live without peripheral vision because it makes me feel so out of control. When I come into a room, I can't see who's in there unless I turn my head from side to side. I could sooner see myself not able to recover some of my other deficits than to be left with limited sight. I try not to think about that possibility because it makes me freak out.

The doctor told me I had made some progress with my visual field. The progress wasn't obvious to me, but the vision field testing showed an increased area of vision. It felt like a weight had been lifted.

March 27, 2022

I'm proud to report that my memory is coming back. Take astrology. Before my stroke, I knew the sign of everyone I met. I knew their moon sign, their rising sign, their Venus, and their Mercury. At work, I would use this knowledge to better understand why people related to each other the way they did.

For example, a sales associate and a manager both had the same sign, but they were so different from each other. One was hopelessly disorganized, always losing things like her glasses (which were usually sitting on top of her head). The other was very anal, keeping copious color-coded, alphabetized, and annotated lists. At first, the difference between them confused me. Then I realized that the super-organized one was desperately trying to compensate for her inner disorganized self while the other was so deep in her disorganization that she just embraced it.

In any event, I shared these observations with the other managers as we discussed how to get the team to work better together. They were amazed by my astrological insights.

So many other things are coming back to mind. I feel like things are settling and I am stabilizing. I don't know what that means or how to explain it, but I'm beginning to feel a sense of peace and tranquility in my brain.

April 3, 2022

I try to write with my mom every day. She kept great notes about our time in the hospital and in rehab, and those have been really helpful in piecing together our journey.

I love writing and I love writing with her. We talk, she tells me things I wasn't aware of or didn't remember, and then I tell her things she just didn't know. It is incredible to spend this time together. My stroke gave us the gift of time we didn't know we even needed. It's been a blessing.

Sometimes, I sigh when I hear how much sadness everyone went through. It makes me feel heavy. But at the same time, it makes me feel so loved. I know how loved I am, and I am so lucky.

I am going to write this book. It is my destiny. I feel the need to reach out to people, to share my story, to help them and their family get through something like this. Maybe they'll draw some relief from the fact that life goes on, people heal, families come together, sometimes when there's nothing they can even agree on.

David

Though we were months out, I still thought about Jenny continuously when I wasn't with her. It would always make me feel better to text her a heart or some silly emoji. The best time of the day was when I got home and got to kiss her and sniff her head. There was nothing like her big smile as she squeezed my hand.

Caryn

On my half-birthday, April 5th, I sat writing with Jenn and asked her what I could show for the past six months. I'm getting older, and I am more conscious than ever of the passage of time.

I told her it was strange because I would usually measure my life by the concrete accomplishments I could show at work and in my personal life. I hadn't had many of those over the preceding six months. My time had been spent being rather than doing, which feels strange. I have always been a big doer.

But my being had been with Jenn—talking to her, kissing her, holding her hand, looking into her eyes, marveling at her strength and courage, breathing in her amazing resilience. When we were together, everything moved so slowly and evenly that it felt like time wasn't moving. I relaxed into these moments.

Early on, I envisioned Jenn's recovery as an ant crossing a football field, but my understanding shifted. Her recovery was also our recovery. We were all ants crossing the field with her.

Were someone to ask me what I'd been up to for the past six months, I'd say that I was walking hand-in-hand with Jenn, Amanda, David, and Mischa, as a loving family making our way across a sometimes treacherous and sometimes navigable pass, step-by-step and with intention. When I thought about it that way, I realized I'd done more in these sacred six months than in my entire life.

Jenn

April 9, 2022

My friend reached out to do a vision board with me. She thought it would be a good idea to help me set my intentions for the season ahead. I prepared by meditating on what I wanted to bring into this new chapter in my life.

I saw myself walking in tall grass on a sunny day, carrying a bunch of pink roses and white peonies in my hand. Then I started dancing in the field. I imagined myself speaking eloquently and fluently, not trapped by sometimes-incoherent language. I wrote the name Mischa in the rays of the bright sun. He is my bright sun.

I described to her all that I wanted to create in this new phase of my life. And as we spoke on Zoom, she began to design my vision on a large board with markers. It was the most beautiful thing I'd ever seen.

She wrote the words *Rebirth*, *Renewal*, and *Recovery* across the top of the board. She inscribed other affirmations I could repeat to myself. She printed a photo of me from right before my stroke—at a time when I was looking and feeling like my best self—and she put it on the bottom left corner of the board.

I left this experience feeling so motivated. I know I have to live up to the vision that arose from within my soul.

Caryn

A constant presence and source of comfort throughout this entire odyssey was our rabbi. He reached out immediately after Jenn's stroke and asked if he could visit. He never stopped visiting. He saw her in the ICU, while she was on the neuro floor, during her rehabilitation at Glen Cove Hospital, and when she got home. He was a source of calm and a beloved confidante.

Other than Mischa, Amanda, David, and me, Rabbi was the only other person who saw us at our very worst with Jenn clinging to life. He knew how close we came and how far we'd come, and that shared knowledge will tie us together forever.

At the end of each visit, he placed his hands on Jenn's head and recited the Mi Shebeirach, the Jewish prayer for healing, in Hebrew:

> May the One who blessed our ancestors—Abraham, Isaac, and Jacob, Sarah, Rebecca, Rachel, and Leah—bless and heal Jennifer Goldman.
>
> May the Holy Blessed One overflow with compassion upon her, to restore her, to heal her, to strengthen her, to enliven her.
>
> The One will send her speedily, a complete healing—healing of the soul and healing of the body—along with all the ill among the people of Israel and all humankind, soon, speedily, without delay, and let us all say: Amen!

Each time, I placed one hand on Jenn's head and the other on the rabbi. I closed my eyes and let the words carry me like a bird ascending to the heavens. And for that moment, I transcended the pain and was at peace.

David

Jenny had a visit with a well-respected neurosurgeon who had been advising us throughout her stroke in mid-April. He hadn't seen Jenny when she was a patient at North Shore, but he had followed her case closely and was readily available for consultation and support.

It was an emotional visit. When he came into the consultation room, he said he had spent the last fifteen minutes reviewing Jenny's chart and most recent scans.

"Jenn is a walking miracle," he said. "The neurosurgeon and entire team at North Shore hit a home run in their treatment. You are going to continue to recover."

I saw tears in his eyes as he told us this type of recovery just doesn't happen, and he was grateful to be a part of it. He expressed how amazing it was for a neurosurgeon to witness such a result.

His words were just what we all needed to hear. Jenny's face beamed. How lucky we were.

Amanda

April 15th was my birthday, and I was not in the mood to celebrate. With so much loss and sadness and trauma over the past year, I was still having a hard time with it all. Jenn, though, was doing amazing. I was so glad to see her every day and watch her progress.

Jenn

April 16, 2022

I'm embarrassed to say I had a temper tantrum last night that went into a full-blown panic attack. The tantrum was awful, like an explosion erupted within me that scorched my insides. I doubled over like I had taken a punch to my stomach. My entire body turned bright red as if I were on fire. It felt like I was being squeezed from the inside out. My fists clenched, my face tightened, and an intense rage caused me to spew venomous anger at my mom.

I feel so much shame for the tantrum. People my age shouldn't be having them, although as my mom says, people my age shouldn't be having strokes either. She's right that I shouldn't judge myself, considering all I've been through. It's hard, though. I'm a perfectionist and I'm really tough on myself.

The tantrum set in as I was speaking, and I suddenly couldn't find my words. Words have always come easily to me. I love them for their ability to capture my feelings. They are my favorite form of expression. I speak to people, motivate them, connect with them through the stories I tell. To now struggle to find words is horrible and terrifying.

I'm scared I won't get my words back. I try to calm myself by staying present.

April 17, 2022

The movement in my right shoulder is still restricted. My right arm and hand are very weak because I really haven't been able to use them with my shoulder locked in place. I am going to have another round of Botox injections shortly to free up my shoulder.

Once that happens, I'm hoping I will be able to move my right arm, which will permit me to use my right hand more easily.

In the meantime, I'm supposed to use my right hand and arm as best as I can. But that's been really difficult to do.

It's unbelievable to think about all the steps that go into using my right arm, how many hundreds of nerves have to trigger, muscles have to move, blood has to flow, in addition to the coordination, balance, and emotional confidence.

First, I move my whole body forward. Second, I lean in and move toward what I want to grab. Next, I drag it toward me. Then, wrapping my fingers around it as best as I can, I slowly pick it up. Even the lightest object feels so heavy. I worry about dropping it. It is a slow, agonizing process.

But I will do it again and again, pushing through the pain, frustration, and resistance. Repetitive actions build connections. That's what neuroplasticity is all about, and I am completely determined to heal.

Caryn

There is a young dogwood tree just outside the side door to our house. It's about two or three years old, and it is magnificent. I love dogwoods because they are beautiful every season. In the spring and summer, their blossoms are fragrant and delicate. In the fall, their leaves turn a deep green. In the winter, the bark's browns and beiges glisten in the sun.

I was searching for the strength to go on, to take it day by day, to be able to be a support to my family, to be upbeat, to carry them when they were not able to carry themselves these last seven months. I thought it would help to have a visual anchor I could call upon to remind me of my strength. One night when I was outside it occurred to me the young dogwood tree could be my anchor.

For the last seven months, I visited that tree every single night. Before bed, I would open the door, shut all the outside lights, and study the tree, carefully observing its young, strong roots. Its elegant boughs stretched upward like open arms reaching to the heavens. I thought about how trees are the ultimate survivors, withstanding the rains, the cold, the snow, the bright sun, and the winds. Each day, though, it was still there, strong and true, reaching upward.

I tried to see myself as the trunk of that dogwood. I was powerful. I could do this. Whatever happened, I was ready with gratitude and an open heart.

Jenn

April 21, 2022

I continue to feel frustrated with my inability to speak the way I used to. The thoughts don't come fluently, and the words stay stuck inside of me. I'm embarrassed to speak to anyone because I feel like a fool.

My speech therapist has been telling me the way to overcome it is to get out and practice speaking as much as I can. That's why tonight, I wanted to make a toast at dinner. When everyone was seated at the table, I said I wanted to speak. Everyone was amazed and excited, and they encouraged me to go ahead.

I started to speak but soon lost my way. I couldn't find the words and I became agitated and fidgety. The sensation in my chest made me think about what it would feel like to be stuck on a roller coaster up in the air. I was unable to breathe and panic set in. I stopped speaking midway through the toast, and although everyone complimented me at the table for my first toast since my stroke, I felt embarrassed and frustrated. I wasn't hopeless, though.

My mom said something about how perfectionism is inconsistent with healing. I knew what she meant. I've always been so hard on myself.

I sat and quietly ate my dinner and mulled over what I had intended to say. The next moment, I got up, asked everyone to quiet down, and I proceeded to give the toast—not the best version I might one day be able to give, but a version. Even though I still ended up feeling that I hadn't done well, it felt brave to make another attempt at the toast. As frustrated and agitated as I might become, I am not going to quit.

April 22, 2022

I don't think I could have done this without the love and support of Mischa, who's been here for me every single day since this happened. He's been a rock for me, a grounding force. His love for me is absolute and steadfast. He is kind, gentle, yet strong. He soothes me, and has boundless patience with me, helping transfer me from my wheelchair to the bed or commode.

It's strange being thirty-one and needing to have your boyfriend move you into and out of a wheelchair. It's certainly more than Mischa bargained for. Yet, he remains so committed to me throughout everything. I am thankful for his love.

April 23, 2022

My vision continues to scare me. It's still compromised peripherally. It's just complete blackness in those places where there used to be images. Originally, I couldn't see anything above or below my face, so I guess there has been improvement.

It is still frightening though. To be in a room and not be able to see but hear the sounds around me leaves me feeling claustrophobic and completely out of control, especially when it's a noisy room or I'm in a public setting.

The visual field testing I'm doing shows some improvement. It's not coming fast enough for me, so I've started to do weekly vision training with a neuro-optometrist. She's great and has worked with athletes to enhance their sports performance. She's utilizing some of the same programs with me.

Even though everyone tells me to stay patient and just do the work, I often feel that my vision will never return and that scares me when I stay in that mindset. My vision does inhibit me because I don't feel safe going to noisy public places or even to work, which is very upsetting for my mom, who believes being out will help my language and mobility.

April 24, 2022

My aunt isn't ordinarily comfortable sharing her emotions, so it came as a surprise to me when my mom walked in today with a journal my aunt had written for me during the time when I was really sick.

It's written in pencil in a small blue notebook, the size you can carry in your back pocket. "Book 1" is written on the cover.

The journal was meant to fill me in on what was happening during the time I was not present.

As soon as my mom gave it to me, I opened it and thumbed through the pages. Some of the parts were nostalgic and took me back to my childhood. Other parts were funny. Some were sad, even wistful. I could almost hear my aunt considering the possibility that I might not recover, and things might never be the same. The fact that she had to navigate through a sea of worst-case scenarios alone broke my heart.

On September 2, 2021, she wrote: *Hi, My Sweets. Today was another good day. You're breathing on your own. Amazing!! I really think tomorrow you're going to wake up. We all miss you so much. Love you.*

Just amazing.

April 25, 2022

I haven't been able to meditate for about six months because I constantly feel restless, a buildup of energy in the left side of my body, my good side. It's hard to describe, but the sensation keeps me from focusing on meditation.

This doesn't just happen when I'm trying to meditate. It happens all the time, whether I'm sitting in a chair or lying down. The only thing that keeps my foot relatively still is the boot I have to wear at night when I sleep. Because I'm unable to quiet my body, I'm unable to transcend into the concentration required to meditate.

I miss meditating. Before my stroke, I began each day with an hour of meditation. It energized me and allowed me to focus on what was important.

My belief that I will be able to get back into it keeps me going. As for now, I draw energy from the dreams I have that I'll be able to walk again, speak fluently, and use my right hand and arm. The thought of motivating others also revitalizes me. I find it inspiring and uplifting.

Caryn

David and I went with Jenn to Glen Cove Hospital for her appointment with her rehab doctor. We wanted to hear about her progress, of course, but as it was the end of April, it was also time for her to have painful Botox injections in her neck, her inner thigh, and her arm. We wanted to be there to support her.

Even though we were on a different floor, being back at Glen Cove was hard for me. The institutional wall color, lighting, and smell of antiseptic took me back in time. My heart dropped to the floor as soon as we walked in, but I put it away. We were here for Jenn.

We quietly settled in the waiting room outside the doctor's office. Suddenly, I heard music coming from Jenn's phone. Jenn's high-pitched voice broke out into "Livin' La Vida Loca." She was absolutely consumed and genuinely joyful, singing at the top of her lungs, shaking her head from side to side.

I immediately thought back to her very young years. On Sunday mornings, she would dress up in a pink tutu, silver tiara, and white boa. Pretending she was Anna waltzing with the King of Siam or Dr. Henry Higgins dancing with Eliza Doolittle, she would run through the room, wand in hand, uninhibited and undeterred by any reality but her present sense of joy.

I started to tear up, touched by her capacity to be so open. It was a gift to see it again, but it also scared me. *Will she be able to safely navigate the world?* I questioned. The word "safely" bounced around in my head. Didn't vulnerability make you stronger, better able to have real connection? Wasn't her experience richer and more real now?

There were still so many lessons to be learned from this horrific event.

Amanda

Jenn's regular aides were not with us on the weekends, so the agency sent people to fill in. One aide had been filling in for a few Sundays and everything seemed to be working out. Until it wasn't.

My dad and Mischa were out sailing one Sunday and were not going to be back until the evening, so it was just Jenn, my mom, and me home with the aide. The aide had taken Jenn to the bathroom, and when they returned, the aide was angry.

"Your daughter is not doing enough to help me transfer her from the wheelchair to the commode. I am going to injure myself because of her laziness. I am leaving now," the aide proclaimed in a loud voice.

I looked across at my mom whose mouth had dropped open in sheer disbelief. I could see she was getting angry. So was I.

"Perhaps you've forgotten that Jenn had a stroke and that she can't do any more than what she's doing? What am I missing?"

Jenn burst into tears, and I couldn't stay silent. "You don't know Jenn, but she is the hardest worker on earth, and if she could do more, she would."

Grabbing her coat from the chair, the aide replied that she was leaving.

"You mean you're not coming back next Sunday?" my mom asked.

"No. I'm going home. Now."

"How can you leave us like this? It's four o'clock and the evening aide doesn't get here until eight. Amanda and I can't transfer Jenn. We don't have the strength to lift her out of her wheelchair. Is she supposed to pee in her pants?"

"That's not my problem," she said, turning and walking out the front door.

Seeing how upset and scared Jenn was, I pulled my mom to the side.

"We have to make it seem like we have this under control. We just have to figure out whatever we have to figure out. Be positive," I told her.

We put on a good front and Jenn finally calmed down. Everything was going well until Jenn told us around 6 p.m. she had to use the bathroom.

"Can you hold it?" my mom asked.

"I *have* been holding it . . . for like, an hour."

"Oh, Lord," my mom answered.

I jumped in.

"We've got this, Jenn. Don't you worry."

I wheeled Jenn into the bathroom, and when we got there, my mom and I planned out our strategy. I was going to pull Jenn out of the wheelchair and pivot her so that she would be standing over the toilet. There were arms on both sides of the toilet, and she had the strength to stand on her own using the arms for support. My mom would sit on the bathroom floor in front of Jenn and lower her pants. She would pee standing up over the toilet.

As I tried to move Jenn, we both immediately ended up on the floor.

Then my mom started to laugh.

Then we started to laugh.

Hysterically. Uncontrollably.

And then the pee ran down—over Jenn's pants, her underwear, the floor, my leg. It was a pee party. From the floor, we began to think about the impossible tasks of getting her off the floor and cleaning her up. Just as we were going to try another sure-to-fail plan, I heard the garage door open and in walked Dad and Mischa, back early from their sail. *Thank God.* Mischa would be able to get Jenn back to herself.

The whole episode could have been a disaster, but it turned into a great release from the stress we constantly held with us. To be lying together laughing on the bathroom floor was exactly what we needed. I'll never forget it.

David

Jenny started on an online vision restoration therapy program called NovaVision in May. She completed two modules each day, six days a week. She completed three pre-therapy assessment tests that enabled them to establish a baseline for her vision on May 25, 2022. They performed the three tests again on June 23, 2022.

Occupational Therapy Report, 5/25/2022

Good morning, Caryn and Dave,

I wanted to give you an update on Jenny's progress. We are doing a lot of work to provide proprioceptive input to the affected side as well as the unaffected so as to make everything more symmetrical. Yesterday Jenny did work on a Pilates chair where she had to stand in front of the chair and lean forward rounding her back and articulating her spine and pressing down on pedals with resistance. When she stood up I had her facing a mirror, and she did an unbelievable job. We are advancing into new movements. I'm saving time to work on her peripheral vision and cognitive challenges. She is cognitively unbelievable, and we have a great time. I will be starting to use a vision therapy program, one of many that I have for her to work on. I wanted to keep you posted; call me with any questions or concerns.

Jenn

June 1, 2022

Until recently, there's been a thick fog in my brain. Connections, memories, words, associations are there in the front of my brain, but they are swirling around so I've been unable to grasp or hold on to them. It felt like I wasn't connected to the world outside of myself, like I was so deep in my body that it had swallowed me. It was very scary.

People would ask me things I should have known the answer to, but I didn't. It was embarrassing and it left me feeling out of control and afraid to put myself in social situations. It's held me back because I've not been willing to interact with people feeling the way I do.

Thankfully, I'm starting to be able to connect to my past experiences and memories. Little by little, things are getting clearer in my brain. Also, I've started to write everything down, which helps solidify things in my mind. Every day, I write about what I did that day.

Today, for example, it's June 1st and I wrote about the progress I made in May. I walked for the first time with the walker and without anyone helping me. My physical therapist told me if I did it once, I can do it again. I also have more coherent thoughts. My voice is stronger, my right arm is more flexible. I feel good about my progress.

David

Since her stroke, Jenny has been struggling with her working memory. Working memory is a skill that lets us hang on to important information until we need it, like having a temporary note stuck to our brain that reminds us to do things like buy milk from the store. A stroke interferes with the brain's ability to hold on to that information, and that's why Jenny loses her train of thought when she is telling a story or explaining something.

Fortunately, the brain can rewire itself and that process is activated through practicing a certain skill consistently and very often. The more you exercise your memory, the better your memory will get.

Jenn

June 16, 2022

My dad has always been a perfectionist who laughs off his emotions, but then sighs repeatedly as if we don't understand that his sighs are an expression of his fear. His sighs are scary and make things worse. I wish he could just say what he was feeling.

Recently, there's been a shift in the way he communicates that is almost incredible. With my lack of peripheral vision, for example, he has taken a calm, supportive approach. He tells me we will take things one step at a time, and we will be able to handle whatever comes our way because that's the only thing we can do.

I've never seen him accept the fact that he has no control. But that's what he's doing here. And his willingness to open up his heart to me is a responsibility I will honor. His making himself vulnerable is beautiful and is an expression of his deep love.

June 17, 2022

I'm feeling scared because I had two more seizures this past Sunday. I feel like I can have another one at any time and that terrifies me. When I'm having one, I'm completely out of control. I know everything that's happening, but I have no ability to stop myself. I'm writhing on the floor. My eyes are closed, and I can't open them. People are shouting at me. It is pure chaos.

My dad gets really freaked out. He gets into my face and tries to force me to calm down, but I can't. I know it's scary for him, but it's frustrating because I can't calm down. Mischa is very calm when I'm seizing.

These seizures make me nervous because they come out of nowhere. There are no symptoms I can connect them with, and I have no notice before they happen. The seizure specialist explained the seizures were coming from the part of my brain where I had my stroke, which is not unusual. He is trying to stop the seizures with medication, but there are no guarantees. It's a matter of trial and error to figure out what medication or combination of medications might work. It's just really upsetting.

June 21, 2022

I've done a lot of thinking about how it feels to have a very visible physical disability that causes me to be in a wheelchair. I've always taken my mobility for granted, and never imagined I'd be in this situation. But here I am, in it.

I feel so vulnerable and exposed.

I've believed from the beginning I will walk again. That's not the issue. What upsets me is I am no longer able-bodied, which makes me feel unprotected and unsafe in this world. I used to drive all over the country on my own, meet people from all different walks of life, attend festivals and yoga conferences, and even present at these events. Never did I feel unsure of myself or of my ability to take care of myself.

Now, I am completely dependent on others, and it's been really hard for me to accept the physical limitations of this stroke. At the same time, though, these limitations have made me stronger. They contribute to my growth as a person; they make me wiser and more compassionate toward others.

Amanda

We were over ten months out, and I was going through my photos. As I scrolled through the pictures from August of last year, I
began to laugh.

After I got the call to come to the hospital, I drove there like
a deranged person. I had to be with Jenn. I entered the five-level
parking garage, but it was a really busy day, and I couldn't find
any available spaces. Whether there really were none or whether
it was because I was so agitated, I may never know.

I saw a sign that read *Valet Parking* in front of a closed gate, and
at least twenty free spaces on the other side of the gate. I was des-
perate. I didn't think about the fact that those spaces were reserved
for use by valet parkers. It didn't matter anyway. I had to get into
the hospital. I plowed through the gate and parked. I ran past the
broken gate, now on the ground, and into the emergency room.

Two hours later, we were in the waiting room—my dad, my
mom, Mischa, and me. Dr. Woo had just broken the horrible
news that Jenn's condition might not be treatable, and he had just
left the room to do the angiography. We were hanging on for dear
life. Was Jenn going to live or die?

At this moment, I got a text from a towing company: *You are
parked illegally. Your car has been booted. Bring $302 in cash to the
security desk downstairs immediately. We will be here until five.*

I texted back: *I'm waiting to hear if my sister is going to live or die.
I don't have $302 with me. Keep the car.*

They texted a few more times during the day—which, when I
thought about it, was really crazy. I ignored them all.

The next day, when Jenn was finally stabilized and in the
NICU, my dad and I went downstairs to the security office to

find out about the car. As soon as my dad began to explain, the person on duty interrupted him.

"That's you who crashed through the gate? What were you thinking? We have it on camera. Everyone in security has seen it," he said, laughing.

At the time, I was so embarrassed and angry that people found humor in an event so stressful to me that I crashed my car through a gate and knocked it off its hinges. Not knowing whether Jenn would live or die, none of us found it funny at the time. But after all these months, I can even understand why the security team was entertained.

I cracked up all over again.

Caryn

I started to notice a new innocence about Jenn. It was different from the emotional lability I'd been concerned about previously. That was due to injury to her neural pathways that regulate emotional expression. Rather, I was now seeing an unguarded openness that came from a place of strength and self-acceptance.

It was like the vault door to her heart had suddenly blown open. The defenses she formed early in her life seem to no longer serve her. She seemed to have evolved into a more connected, authentic person. A good friend of Jenn's from college came to visit. Before she left, she said Jenn was softer and lighter, with less of an edge—that Jenn seemed to have connected to her inner child. This was the perfect way to capture my own perspective.

Jenn asked me if I thought she had lost her filter. I was quietly overjoyed by her question because it reflected the return of her pre-stroke intuitiveness, but more important, it spoke to a shift in the way she viewed her place in the world from one of vulnerability to one of strength.

"What do you mean by that?" I asked. I knew what she was getting at, but I wanted her to try to explain it.

"Is it appropriate to tell my speech therapist that I love her or my occupational therapist that he was a good person? Does that make people feel uncomfortable? I've lost my sense of things, and I just can't tell."

"Well, so here's the question. How do you feel when you share these feelings with people?"

"Free and amazing," Jenn answered.

"There you go. Never question what comes from your heart. Being vulnerable with your feelings is the most powerful thing you can do. Don't stop now."

David

The results of Jenny's visual field test came back on June 23rd, and they showed progress. When stimulus strength is high, accuracy is high and response time is fast; when stimulus strength is low, accuracy is low and response time is slow.

With Jenny's right eye, there was a 10 percent increase in her stimuli accuracy, a decrease in her response time, and a 4.7 percent increase in her fixation accuracy. With her left eye, there was a 10.2 percent increase in her stimuli accuracy, a decrease in her response time, and a 0.4 percent increase in her fixation accuracy.

The reviewer praised Jenny for her high level of attention

to the program and for the results she achieved. Jenny reserved judgment, cautious about not getting too excited.

I was enthusiastic. Her progress would continue.

Jenn

June 18, 2022

For the last six weeks, I've been doing nonstop reading on neuroplasticity, which is the brain's ability to rewire itself by forming new neural pathways and restoring others. MRIs and new scientific tools that image the brain have provided neuroscientists with a better understanding of how the brain heals itself and grows on a daily basis.

A few things I find amazing: The brain is continuously rewiring itself. In other words, washed-away pathways can be reformed and sometimes end up being more efficient than they were before being washed away. Also amazing are the things you repeatedly tell yourself. These mantras form neural networks in your brain and become your new way of thinking and being. Telling myself I have the strength to deal with whatever comes my way lays the groundwork for believing it, and believing it causes me to feel it, and feeling it causes me to have it. It's crazy but it's also amazing. I've been spending about an hour a day working on positive thinking and self-talk.

June 23, 2022

Today, I had neuropsych testing. My speech therapist thought it would be a good idea so they could assess where I am and how to best help me move forward.

I was stressed about it. I'm a perfectionist and I knew going into it that no matter how I did, I'd end up feeling bad about my performance. Also, I used to do motivational speaking, and I'm hoping to do it again. I want to share my story. I'm not ready to hear that my skills are not strong enough for me to do that.

The testing involved memory, the ability to match patterns to determine shapes and colors, and other stuff I found annoying. The memorization was the worst part. I was asked to memorize some random words and then they would introduce some unrelated idea to throw me off, and then I had to repeat the random words.

The testing took two hours and was really hard. I became so frustrated that at one point I put my head down on the table and told the person administering the test I couldn't do it. She encouraged me to continue, and I did, although I honestly felt like I didn't have a choice.

While I first felt relief when it ended, I soon became angry. The test reminded me of a standardized high school exam that measures cognitive skills and abilities but doesn't measure passion, mindset, energy, or any of the real things that you need to succeed in life and, in my case, fully recover.

I don't want to be defined by objective skills that put me someplace on a chart. From day one, I have beaten the odds. I'm alive. A neurosurgeon told me I was a walking miracle. A part of that is luck, but a bigger part is attitude, spirituality, gratitude, and the love and support of my family. If anything is going to get me to recover, it's that.

So, I don't want people to measure me by the objective cognitive qualities the testing reveals. I want them to look at my entire skill set, including the drive and determination I have to fully recover. Then set their goals high enough to get me there.

June 30, 2022

I started working with a massage therapist who is very spiritual. She did a Vedic birth chart reading and breakdown for me. A birth chart shows the position of the whole cosmos at the date, time, and place of my birth. It can help me understand the deeper aspects of my personality and character.

My main planet is Jupiter, which represents the giver, the helper, and the teacher. Those qualities resonate with me because I believe my purpose is to share my story with people so they may feel less alone in every aspect of their lives. My career is represented by Mars, which stands for intensity. I take that to mean I would be sharing truth with people, piercing through the protective veil they wear.

My physical body is represented by Venus, which includes the adorning of self. My grandmother always told me to listen to my body and take care of it. I think she'd be proud of all I am doing to support myself through this recovery.

My creative play is represented by Mercury. This includes self-study, using senses, questioning, and discovering. I am very inquisitive, and I love to discover things about nature and people. I feel like a child because of how excited I get when I come to understand things.

The reading confirmed the qualities I knew I had but, more important, made me feel confident about my path.

July 10, 2022

Today is my two-year anniversary with Mischa. Two years ago today, I drove from Snowmass, Colorado, to Brooklyn, New York, to meet him in person. We had been communicating on the phone for two and a half months, but COVID kept me in Colorado. We talked for hours. I found him to be intuitive and strong, but also soft and gentle. When I finally met him, we fell deeply in love. One year and one month after we met, I had my stroke. That anniversary is also approaching.

Almost half of the time we've spent together I have been incapacitated to some degree. He has stood by me through everything. I can feel his love in the way he looks at me, the way he supports my back when I walk, the way he puts my leg brace on, the way he takes me to the bathroom, the way he dresses me—his love has been a lifeline.

And now, with our anniversary, I'm feeling sad, like I am letting Mischa down. He doesn't say that at all. I feel like I'm not able to give him what he needs right now. I feel he would want to be married, live with me alone, sleep in the same bed as me, have me work and be independent, maybe start to think about beginning a family and a life together. I am so sad because I cannot give him any of that and I don't know when I'll be able to.

My feelings about disappointing Mischa make me even more frustrated with the slow pace of my progress. When he sees me crying, he tells me he's sad for me. He says I'm the one who has lost everything and that he will be here. I believe him, but I still feel a loss for the life we would be having if not for this stupid stroke.

It's been almost one year. One year ago, I was in a hospital bed with tubes all over my body. I couldn't eat, breathe, or regulate any of my bodily functions without machines. I was in and out of consciousness and didn't remember how to play tic-tactoe. I tried to put my hand through the iPad screen to pet Luna. I was a mess.

I can do all those things I couldn't now, and I am grateful. But I need to do more and be more for me and for him. And I need to do it now. There has been so much loss for me this year and I need to acknowledge that as well as acknowledge my progress. My progress doesn't diminish my sense of loss.

My mom asked me how I can manage the feelings of loss. I told her I just have to cry it out. I'm okay with that, and so is she.

Caryn

We were approaching the year mark, and every moment of Jenn's day was focused on healing. When she wasn't in her therapies, she was reading about neuroplasticity and doing self-talk exercises to support the rewiring of her brain. She read that people who think positively generate more neurons in their prefrontal cortex, which translates into the formation of new pathways. Repetition is a key ingredient in the creation of these new pathways.

Jenn downloaded an affirmation app on her phone and began to play it at least five times a day. The session narrator's voice was hypnotic, and he spoke in threes. He repeated each statement three times, emphasizing a different word in the statement with each repetition.

"I *like* who I am. *I* like who I am. I like who *I* am."

As soon as she downloaded it, Jenn embraced it fully, so inspired by it all. I admired her focus on healing, but for me, it was mind-numbing. Every time his voice started to drone, I felt like the subject of unwelcome indoctrination in a dystopian novel.

To each our own.

Jenn

July 21, 2022

I practice positivity every single day. These are my affirmations:

1. I skip down the aisle of my wedding with my dad. Our arms are interlocked. We are dancing to "Just the Two of Us." It's such a joyful moment.

2. I marry Mischa, the love of my life. We are so happy together.

3. My body and brain are fully healed. They are the pinnacle of health and well-being. I walk, run, skip, and jump wherever I go.

4. I dance again. I move with passion and intensity.

5. I work out hardcore. I do crunches, planks, side planks, sit-ups. I do anything and everything I want to.

6. I live on my own with Mischa. We live in a house on the north shore of Long Island.

7. I have two kids with Mischa—one girl and one boy. The boy's name is Noah. The girl's name is Layla. They are healthy and happy. We have a beautiful family who is a perfect astrological match.

8. I see fully, clearly, and sharply out of my periphery.
9. I am a motivational speaker. I speak on stages across the globe. I inspire millions of people everywhere.
10. I write a successful book that is translated into hundreds of languages. It becomes the focus of what I speak about.

I'm not there yet. But I'm happy. I still have my ambitions, my hopes and dreams, a purpose to fulfill. And I will get there.

July 22, 2022

I was able to sink into a deep meditation today. It was very exciting because I haven't been able to meditate in months. I lay on my back on my couch with my hand on my chest. The other palm faced down because I can't face it up right now. I set a timer for ten minutes and just started breathing. Amazingly, my left leg was quiet. Using sound as an anchor to the present moment, I moved into it. I didn't resist it or push it away. The next thing I knew, my alarm rang, and I realized I had meditated.

I don't know what allowed me to get into it today, but I'm thankful.

Caryn

Not a day has gone by without my giving thanks that Mischa came into our lives. Mischa came to us on the night of Jenn's stroke and has been living with us ever since. He has been an angel, and we could not have gotten by without his constant, calm, warm, and loving presence. He has been a good friend to Amanda, having steadied and supported her time and time again. He has been a light to Jenn.

I think back to the qualities Jenn included on her manifestation board. She wanted her partner to have a "big golden heart," to be "kind and generous," to be "comfortable being vulnerable," to be "authentic," and to be able to "share his feelings and emotions." All these things were Mischa from the beginning—soft and strong, honest and open, a profoundly beautiful soul.

I do worry about how much he can take. Certainly, this was a lot more than he anticipated. I feared this would all become too much of a burden for him. If that ever became the case, I would understand, but it made me sad to think about it.

Jenn

July 23, 2022

I hate that my memory is impaired. I went to work the other day for an hour and sat in on a meeting. When I started to speak, I completely lost my train of thought and froze. It was embarrassing, and I felt like everyone was judging me.

My speech therapist says I have to continue to work on regaining my working memory and that memory-intensive rehab exercises are really important and helpful to that end. I hate doing them because they seem stupid, and I just can't see any connection between my doing them and my memory improving. The other day, though, Mom showed me some articles on the importance of rehab exercises and so I'm now less resistant. I downloaded an app on my phone with some exercises. I've been trying to practice twice each day. I am also trying to maintain an appointment calendar, keep a daily to-do list, and write. I'm always making notes in my phone, and that is a big help.

If I want to do motivational speaking, though, I'm going to have to fully restore my working memory. I am determined.

July 24, 2022

Perfectionism has plagued me my entire life. When I was young, I would purposely not try my hardest in school because I didn't want to disappoint myself if I didn't get the best grade. I'm generally a competitive person, but I don't like to compete because it makes me feel bad about myself, like I'm not good enough.

I'm also very perfectionistic about my recovery. If I don't do well in therapy for the day, I get upset with myself and stay upset for the rest of the day. It gets in the way of me seeing my progress. Sometimes I only look at how far from full recovery I am.

My therapist and I have been working on this a lot.

"Can you just accept yourself for being the imperfect person that you are?" she finally said to me in a session.

I cried. I can't accept myself. I don't know if I will ever be able to.

We did EMDR—a type of somatic therapy where you try to get relief from traumatic memories that are stored away in your body—around these thoughts and with it came a big release. It was intense, but it can really help to bring things to the surface. I cried a lot. I got very hot and tingly. My arms vibrated. And by the end, I felt a weight had been lifted.

Obviously, I'm not done with perfectionism. I'm just going to try to talk to myself differently about it. I'm going to tell myself that I'm okay as I am, that I deserve love, and that I have the ability to love others. If I can stay focused on those things, I will be free.

July 25, 2022

My neuro-optometrist told me my eyes were getting better. She could tell because I wasn't moving my head side to side as much when doing the exercises.

I do and don't believe her.

Caryn

Jenn and I talked about how it feels to be approaching the one-year mark since the stroke. Like Jenn, I thought we'd be much further along in her healing at this point. I thought she'd be walking, using her right arm completely, showering on her own, without a night aide, maybe even working a few days a week, or maybe having started her career as a motivational speaker. I imagined she would be living in her own apartment with Mischa, that she would be back on track, that her life would be more fully normalized.

We were so far from where we were, but we were still so far from the place we wanted to get to. It was hard to come to terms with. It was so sad to think about how much more work there was to do without any estimated completion date. I knew Jenn would achieve her recovery goals, but the path was feeling less clear to me.

I used to think of her as an ant trying to cross a football field, slowly but steadily making its way through the elements, head down, determined, unstoppable. We knew where we needed to get to, and it was just a matter of staying the course. After so long, it felt like we were traveling together through a thick forest, the trees and dense foliage making it impossible to see beyond it or to determine the route we needed to take.

I tried to stay grounded in the belief that wherever we emerged, Jenn would choose to make the best of it, to be grateful for her progress, and to never stop pushing further and further. And I would be right there with her, following her lead, taking my cue from her, meeting her where she is, deferring to her mindset.

Jenn

August 5, 2022

Today, I lifted my right leg from my knee. On my own. Without anyone helping me. It was exhilarating. I kept repeating the process to make sure I hadn't imagined it, and it really had happened. I was scared I wouldn't be able to do it again, and I got more and more excited as I was able to repeat the movement.

My physical therapist was the one who got me to lift my leg. He recommended that my dad buy an electrical stimulation device. He thought it would be really helpful. I wasn't sure because the one that I used when I got out of the hospital seemed to do nothing. But when the device arrived, I did the stimulation for ten to fifteen minutes. Immediately, I was able to move my leg and engage my thigh, which had been asleep up until that moment.

Mischa videoed me lifting my leg and was able to capture my uninhibited joy. The fact that I've been able to accomplish this makes me feel very hopeful about my progress. I understand this didn't happen overnight, and even though I was able to see the results in a moment, I know these results were a product of continued hard work every single day. I feel more optimistic than ever. I am going to recover.

You never know what each day of recovery and life will bring. You can choose to be negative and discouraged or you can try to be hopeful and open. Who knows what progress lies in store for tomorrow?

Caryn

One of my great joys has been to go into Jenn's room first thing in the morning when she has just woken up. I usually find her lying on her bed, her legs and arms being stretched by Shanelle, her incredible aide who has become like another daughter to us. Her eyes are closed, and she is somewhere between wakefulness and sleep, her body gently rising and falling as she breathes. She is unguarded and unafraid and that amazes and inspires me. In those moments, I feel like I am in the presence of something boundless and profound. The power of that connection is magical.

I approach her, gently kiss the top of her head, and take in her scent. She smells like her rich aromatic concoction of rosehip seed oil, jojoba oil, and rose essential oil, which she applies every night before bed. It smells luscious.

I sit down on the bed next to her. She knows I'm there for our morning ritual. I gently ask her the same two questions I've been asking her for months now, and she then follows with her question to me and my response.

"Good morning, lovie. How did you sleep?"

"I slept really well, Mom."

A huge smile fills her face, and the beauty of the moment knocks me out. She's so peaceful, so accepting, so open and reachable. It makes me want to cry.

"Did you have any dreams?"

"No. I still haven't had dreams since the stroke."

Her voice is one of neutral acceptance, reflecting neither disappointment nor elation. And then she asks me the question she always asks, the third part of our morning ritual.

"Can we write today, Mom?"

"Yes, I'd really love that."

The ritual gave me the chance to watch her as she navigated the dialectic between accepting her present limitations while at the same time pushing relentlessly for full recovery. What courage that required. It was an exquisite thing to bear witness to.

10

ONE YEAR AND COUNTING

Jenn

August 18, 2022

Today is the one-year anniversary of my stroke, and I have some reflections on this past year. The tragedy of my stroke has been such a blessing for our family. It's been a gift.

It's brought our family closer in ways I never could have imagined. It's made us stronger. It's bonded us. No one knows what we've had to overcome. No one can or will ever know.

I'm so grateful for this period of time and I will look back on it fondly. It's honestly been the best period of my life. It's freed me. It's made me step into myself and completely shed my armor.

It's remarkable how something so horrible can be such a blessing, but that's what this has truly been. I'm very thankful.

Amanda, you are my ride-or-die, absolute best friend in the whole world.

Mom, you are my protector, my champion, the one who looks out for me and who always has my back.

Dad, you are my superhero, my inspiration, the one I want to be like and impress.

Mischa, you are my forever man. I am incredibly grateful and excited about your role in my life.

August 21, 2022

We had a large family gathering today for my thirty-second birthday. Friends and family came by—all the people who had supported me and my family this past year. At one point, my mom asked for silence, and everyone circled up and gave me their attention.

I spoke.

"Thank you, everyone, for being here on this momentous occasion. We are gathered to celebrate my life, which was almost taken a year and three days ago to the day. So much happens in a year. So much loss and so much growth. So much letting go—of the layers of perfectionism and self-doubt—at least that's what it's been for me.

"This has been such a hard year. I never thought I would have to rely on someone to help me with showering, walking, and taking care of myself in general. But I will not stop pushing myself until I've reached the top. It's not in my nature to give up.

"I want to thank you all for standing by my side throughout this entire journey. Your outpouring of love has been greatly appreciated and has played a role in my continued recovery. My mom has shared with me what I can only imagine barely scratches the surface of what you must have been feeling. The fear. The not knowing. But I don't want to dwell on that now.

"I want to recognize my perseverance. I want to honor my strength. My hard work and resilience in the face of adversity. And mostly, I want to celebrate my life. This is not just about my birthday. It's about all of you, for standing by my side.

"This year has been a gift. It's a blessing to know that I am alive. I am incredibly grateful for my life."

Caryn

A month after Jenn's thirty-second birthday, we had a follow-up visit with her neuro-ophthalmologist to check her progress. We were hopeful because Jenn's NovaVision therapy work she did twice a day showed slow but steady improvement, especially on her left side.

After three hours of tests, he called us into his consultation room.

"Jenn's peripheral vision is not going to return, although there might be slight improvement," he said matter-of-factly. "And you will never drive again."

Tears filled her eyes, and I thought I was going to die. She had her whole life ahead of her. How could she continue to live on Long Island and not be able to drive? When she said her neuro-optometrist was working on prism glasses, he dismissed the idea, saying they wouldn't help.

No opening, no path forward, no recommendations, nothing. It was like he flattened her with a sledgehammer. It felt mean and unnecessary. I thought back to the words doctors often use as they struggle to maintain emotional detachment from their patients, and I thought again about the toll that takes not only on the doctor but on patients as well.

Once we got home, I told David, who immediately came up with a plan. He was going to see what work was being done in the field and make some calls. I could see Jenn breathe again.

We were determined to keep looking for solutions. We would forever.

Jenn

September 2, 2022

I've been trying to go into work on Wednesdays for a bit if I'm feeling up to it. I want to get back into the swing of things, and I know that work will help with my speech and cognition. Before my stroke, I'd do team building at the store and sometimes run morning meetings where I'd talk about mindfulness, yoga, positive psychology, the importance of gratitude, and other motivational topics. Some mornings, I'd lead the staff in a loving-kindness meditation or some yoga poses.

I decided I wanted to try to run a meeting but was nervous about it. I was worried I'd talk way too fast. Since my stroke, I've tended to speed up when I read, and by the time I'm halfway through, it's hard for people to understand what I'm saying. I'd thought about speaking from memory, but I worried I'd get distracted and lose my place. That would be especially embarrassing, because I'd always taken pride in my ability to speak fluidly and connect with the people I was speaking to.

I knew that I had to do it, though. Otherwise, I wasn't going to move forward in my progress.

The morning of the meeting came, and the staff assembled. While I sat waiting for the meeting to begin, some of the staff came up and hugged me, telling me how great it was that I was doing this. I could feel their anticipation and the weight of their expectations as I sat in my wheelchair, or maybe it was just my anticipation and self-imposed perfectionism.

The group fell silent, and I began.

"Hey, everyone. I'm very glad to be here in front of you all. It's been a long time. I want to talk to you today about an important but simple topic. It's about the way that you talk to yourself and the impact this has on who you are and how you lead your life.

"The thoughts you have and the words you say to yourself matter. They shape you and mold your future actions and behaviors. What you tell yourself becomes your reality.

"I'm a good example. If I tell myself I'm never going to walk again, then I'm not going to walk again. I'm not going to keep pushing to do whatever I can to be able to walk. I'm going to give up and stay in this wheelchair for the rest of my life. But if I tell myself I will be able to walk again and I visualize myself walking, it becomes more of a reality, and I will continue to work until I get there.

"Here's what I do to stay positive: I sit quietly and close my eyes. I see myself in a flowy white cotton dress walking through a field of lavender. The purple sprigs dance as the light breeze touches them. I smell their herby, woodsy, sweet aroma, and bend over to pick some. I bring the bunch up to my nose and inhale. I feel exhilarated. I am exhilarated. There is no wheelchair, no walker, no cane, no aide to support me. The sunshine pours down and warms the top of my head. I'm determined to get there."

I stopped for a moment, and I looked out into the group. People were crying, and then I began to cry. I thought about the many things I'd lost control over due to my stroke. I thought about the things I could not presently do. I took a moment to compose myself and wipe away my tears.

But I then thought about how my stroke did not take my attitude and my determination to progress. Nothing could take that away.

Caryn

Hineini is a word from the Old Testament that speaks to the power of presence and the connection that presence permits. Hineini means I am here. I see you. Fully. I understand. My heart is open, and I am ready to receive. The concept is extraordinary.

In her bed at Glen Cove Hospital when Jenn could not speak but her soft eyes opened and told me everything, Hineini. When I took her hand in mine and she squeezed back, Hineini. When she first stood and I stood right in front of her to look into her eyes and she looked back into mine, Hineini. She knew I saw her. She was telling me she trusted me. It was a profound, powerful moment for me.

The more I think about it, the more I realize how spoiled I was that year. I know it sounds crazy, but I was given the chance to spend my time with Jenn and my family, embrace intimacy and connection, and come to see how it can fortify us in the face of profound chaos and trauma.

Jenn talks about the gift of being able to spend time together we didn't even know we needed. For me, the gift was having discovered the power our family had to come together under the most challenging of circumstances, be present for each other, and be able to see, hear, and offer each other the love, compassion, and support needed to come through it. So many gifts, so many lessons, so much love. That's what the last year has been about.

Hineini.

Epilogue

UPWARD AND ONWARD

Jenn

It's impossible to end a story that keeps evolving. Thankfully, I am continuing to recover, day by day, one step at a time. While that's good news for me, it makes it hard to tie things up for you.

I'm happy to report that at this moment, I'm walking with a brace on each leg and a walker. I feel like in a matter of time, I will be walking without any devices to assist me. Who knows where I'll end up? I still have tone remaining in my right leg and I continue to get Botox shots every three months. I still cannot transfer by myself standing to sitting or sitting to standing. I continue to have aides twenty-four hours a day to help me with that.

As for my speech, I'm making great progress. I still freeze from time to time in conversation, but I forgive myself. I try to be kind. I do still worry about being put on the spot, speaking too quickly, and losing my train of thought. I believe that I'll get there. And the fact that I'm able to write this story with my mom is a testament to my discipline and hard work, as well as to the amazing capability of the brain to heal itself.

My right arm is a work in progress. Again, there is still tone and I continue to receive Botox injections to permit me to have more range of motion.

I'm sad to say that my vision is still very limited. While it has improved slightly, I still can't see peripherally or above or below where I am looking. It's so difficult to navigate the world without the ability to see completely, and I often feel out of control.

Despite that, my spirit continues to soar. I'm positive about my future and am hopeful this book will help mothers, daughters, family members—everyone—navigate challenges that may come their way, whether they be medical, emotional, or spiritual. Attitude is everything when it comes to overcoming hardship.

Before parting, I want to share how difficult it is emotionally for me to step away from co-writing this book. It's become the biggest part of my life and an experience I have been so grateful to share with my mom. As I move into independence and ultimately return to my own life away from my family home, I know I will look back on this time with fondness, great love, and a sense of profound gratitude.

And I know I will not be alone.

ABOUT THE AUTHORS

Before her stroke, **Jennifer Rose Goldman**, a 2013 graduate of Skidmore College with a joint degree in religion and philosophy, founded and served as CEO of Essential Rose, an aromatherapy beauty brand that she started in her college dormitory room. Essential Rose packaged and sold teas and skin-care products for inner, rather than outer, beauty. A motivational speaker on wellness and self-care, she created her own content and taught a six-week course called "Lead Your Life." Jenn is passionate about all things spiritual and loves discovering any new modalities she can immerse herself in.

Caryn Meg Hirshleifer is a co-owner of Hirshleifers, a highly successful fifth-generation luxury retail business located in Manhasset, New York, where she serves as General Counsel as well as in the self-described roles of store historian, store philosopher, and staff nurturer. Before that, she worked as an attorney in New York City government, including her time as General Counsel to the New York City Fire Department and, before that, as General Counsel to Mayor Koch's Office of Homelessness. When not at work, Caryn is reading, writing, or practicing riffs on her electric Fender Mustang bass guitar.